22/11/12

Lindsey Agness is the bestselling author of *Change Your Life with NLP*, *Change Your Business with NLP* and *Still 25 Inside*. She is an experienced NLP trainer and consultant, who works with some of the biggest businesses in the country, as well as running courses and seminars for individuals. She is the MD and founder of The Change Corporation, a highly regarded consulting and training company, and she lives in Kent with her two children.

www.thechangecorporation.com
www.lindseyagness.com
www.agewithattitude.co.uk

WHAT LINDSEY'S WEIGHT-LOSS CLIENTS
ARE SAYING ABOUT HER

'I've tried many different ways to lose weight in the past with limited success. With Lindsey I learnt exactly what motivates me, and once I knew which buttons to push, the rest was easy. Over the past year I've lost two stone and feel so much better in every way. And as a bonus I've come out of the process understanding myself a whole lot better. I feel like I can tackle anything!'   SANDY, KENT

'Lindsey helped me to change how I feel about myself – I went from dowdy and overweight to feeling in control and proud of myself. My self-esteem is at an all-time high and I've lost 15 lbs so far. I've stopped dieting and enjoy my new lifestyle.'   KATHERINE, LONDON

'I used many of the exercises in this book to great effect. Lindsey helped me to overcome my food cravings and lose the urge to snack, and I've lost nearly two stone as a result.'   TERRY, ESSEX

'By changing my thought process, I now feel more in control of what I eat and the size of my portions, which has always been my downfall. I've lost 9 lbs already and the weight's still falling off. Thank you, Lindsey!'   NATALIE, HERTFORDSHIRE

'After working with Lindsey, I feel better than I have in a long time. I now eat more sensibly after she helped me lose the urge to snack, and I've learnt to stop eating when I'm full rather than when the plate is empty. My belt buckle has already moved down two notches, which speaks for itself!'   JULIAN, LONDON

Lose Weight
with
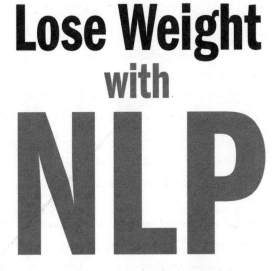

NLP

Be **thinner** and **healthier**
without going on a diet

LINDSEY AGNESS

RODALE

This edition first published 2011 by Rodale
an imprint of Pan Macmillan, a division of Macmillan Publishers Limited
Pan Macmillan, 20 New Wharf Road, London N1 9RR
Basingstoke and Oxford
Associated companies throughout the world
www.panmacmillan.com

ISBN 978-1-90574-487-9

1 3 5 7 9 8 6 4 2

A CIP catalogue record for this book is available from the British Library.

Printed and bound in the UK by CPI Mackays, Chatham ME5 8TD

Visit **www.panmacmillan.com** to read more about all our books and to buy
them. You will also find features, author interviews and news of any author
events, and you can sign up for e-newsletters so that you're always first to
hear about our new releases.

We inspire and enable people to improve their lives and the world around them

In memory of Mary O'Flynn, a vibrant and dynamic spirit who was taken far too abruptly from this universe. Rest happy, Mary.

Contents

Introduction

Whether you've tried every diet out there or you want to lose weight for the first time, this book is for YOU. In fact, this book is for anyone who wants to lose weight and keep it off for ever. It is estimated that nearly 60 per cent of adults want to lose weight. Some are mums wanting their pre-baby figure back; others are older people fighting the gradual thickening around the waist that can come in middle age; others have been struggling with weight gain all their lives, or are yo-yo dieters or binge-eaters. Some people are several stone overweight; others are just feeling a bit plump after overindulging during Christmas or their summer holidays. Whatever your situation, this book will help you to achieve your weight-loss goals, and provide you with the tools to keep the weight off, for good.

That's a big claim to make, so what makes this programme different from the diets you've tried in the past? The difference is that diets are short-term measures that are virtually impossible to maintain permanently, so no matter how much weight you lose, you will no doubt put some or all of it on again, or maybe even more than you lost to start with! This approach, however, works by reprogramming your brain with regard to food, exercise and lifestyle, and once this has been achieved, you will always be able to keep your weight under control.

In this book I will help you to discover your personal attitude towards food, then understand how this has led to your current weight. I will then guide you through the process of changing your thought patterns to enable you to achieve your weight-loss goals and keep the excess pounds off for good.

Dotted throughout the book are 25 simple yet practical exercises that will help you reprogramme your brain so you can change any negative beliefs you have about your weight into positive ones. They'll also help you to discover what type of eater you are, for example, whether you're an Addictive Eater or a Lazy Eater, and will teach you invaluable tools that will help you to stop comfort eating and banish cravings for good. The exercises are an essential component of this book so I encourage you to complete them as fully as possible. You can complete them in this book or, if you prefer, copy them into a personal journal.

It's invaluable to know that you are not alone in your endeavour to lose weight, so in this book I have included case studies of six men and women who I have been working with in a control group to lose weight specifically using the techniques I describe here, as well as the stories of some other weight-loss clients I have worked with over the years. Their results have been remarkable and I will share the secrets of their success with you. You'll be able to learn directly from each of them as they tell us what really made the difference for them, and be able to apply their tips to your own situation. I also share the secrets of other weight-loss clients who have been coached by me in the past so you can learn from them too.

There's no point learning how to control these bad eating habits if you don't then replace them with a better, healthier diet to help you get the best out of your body. Let's face it: you rely on your body for everything so it's important to look after it. It's rather like having a beautiful sports car and putting the wrong fuel in it: it won't work effectively and can even damage the engine. So I will offer you lots of useful tips and advice on how you can become healthier without cutting out everything you love.

The final stage of the programme involves the dreaded E word – exercise! To keep your weight down, the equation is simple: you need fewer calories going in than are going out. However, with so many of us leading hectic lives, eating on the run, working in sedentary occupations and not making time to get our bodies moving, the equation is often the other way round. But don't panic – I'm not going to make you go to the gym five times a week! What I will do, though, is help you to discover things you enjoy that also help you to shed the pounds, whether that's taking long walks in the countryside or learning to salsa. The trick is to find activities that you love to do. I'll show you how to turn your exercise procrastination into motivation to get out there and do something.

You may be wondering who I am to be able to make such ambitious claims? I'm a certified trainer of neuro-linguistic programming – NLP – and aspire to become one of the few female Master Trainers of NLP in the world. NLP is the technique upon which this book is based and it involves reprogramming your mindset to enable you to achieve things you may have previously felt were unattainable. I explain it in more detail in Chapter 1: NLP and Weight Loss.

I'm the author of three best-selling books, *Change Your Life with NLP*, *Change Your Business with NLP* and *Still 25 Inside*, and I run The Change Corporation, through which hundreds of men and women have been trained using NLP techniques. Many of those came to me in the hope of losing weight and went on to achieve great success in their weight-loss goals.

But what makes me uniquely qualified to help you is that I've also been in the position you're in now, and have learned how to use NLP to keep my own weight at a healthy level. I took the skills that I had used in my business to reprogramme the way I thought and felt about myself, build my self-esteem and focus on what I wanted from life. I'm now the ideal weight for my height and feel better than ever before and am excited about sharing my secrets for successful weight loss with you.

So now all that's left to do is to take those first steps on the road to your ideal weight!

NLP and Weight Loss

S o how will NLP help you to lose weight?

NLP is a technique that works by changing your mindset, focusing and motivating you until you believe you can achieve whatever it is you want, in this case weight loss. It empowers you to face your weight challenges head-on and gives you the necessary tools to transform yourself.

In the early 1970s, a linguist, John Grinder, and a mathematician, Richard Bandler, studied individuals who were the best in the world at what they did to find the answer to the question: 'What makes the difference between *world-class* and *mediocre* performance?' They discovered that those people who were at the very top of their professions all held the same sense of self-belief and positive, can-do attitude, whereas people who only performed averagely tended to rely more on luck than judgement! Grinder and Bandler proved that there is a clear relationship between our brains, the language we use and the results we are able to achieve. From their observations, they were able to create strategies and techniques to help others achieve fast and sustainable results in various areas of their lives. They called this approach to change 'Neuro-Linguistic Programming', or NLP, and since then hundreds of thousands of people's lives have been changed permanently using this technique.

You might ask why NLP has been so successful. Unlike other approaches that tell you WHAT you need to do, NLP is a HOW-TO technology, meaning you are not just following a set of instructions – *you* are in control of the changes you are making. For most people, things happen and they react instinctively at a subconscious level. However, NLP gives you the tools to react differently by choice, to become more aware of your thoughts, feelings and behaviour. You will then be ready to take responsibility for your health and fitness once and for all. You will also be able to apply the tools you learn in this book to other areas of your life, such as your career or relationships.

Let's now look at each element of NLP in turn and I'll explain what it's all about and how it will help you to lose weight.

Neuro

Neuro is all about what we **THINK.**

We have over 60,000 thoughts a day and it's our thoughts about food that determine our eating habits, good and bad. Restrictive diets don't stop these thoughts and associated feelings, which is why they don't work – our emotions will always end up overcoming logical, rational thoughts. For example, even if you have lost a few pounds, if that voice inside your head is constantly telling you 'I can't lose weight' or 'I don't look good', it's hardly surprising that you give up trying to lose weight as you believe there's no point.

Your brain is very clever and sets out to get you whatever you focus on. For example, if I say to you, 'Don't think about a blue elephant', what happens? Exactly. The same works for weight. So if you focus on what you don't want ('I don't want to be fat'), your focus is still on being fat, so *being fat* is what you get. However, the opposite is also true. If you carry a positive image of yourself in your thoughts and are excited about your future, you will feel much better about yourself and will be much more motivated to achieve what you want.

It is more complex than this, but the critical point is this: we *can* control our thoughts. I will show you how to get rid of any negative thought patterns you have and replace them with the positive message 'I'm going to do whatever it takes to become fit and healthy for the rest of my life.'

Linguistic

Linguistic is all about what we **SAY**, both verbally and non-verbally.

Like our thoughts, our language also drives how we feel and how we behave. Do you describe your relationship with food as 'difficult, hard work, impossible, a battle'? If you say, 'I can't eat that' or 'I must not have it', you are likely to want it even more because your mind will focus on it. Similarly, if you say, 'I'll try to lose weight' or 'I wish I could lose weight', do you think you'll actually do it? No, because you're telling yourself you have no power to make it happen. In contrast, if you replace these words with 'I will', 'I know', 'I can', 'I am', you immediately move into a more empowered position where you are in control. If you start to change phrases like 'I can't' with 'I choose not to' or 'it's hard to lose weight' with 'it's possible to lose weight', you will begin to believe that you can lose weight and that you will succeed. I'll show you how to do this.

Programming

Programming is all about what we DO.

We are all running programmes, which determine the way we behave, in all areas of our lives all of the time. For example, we run programmes to get up in the morning and travel to work on time (or not!). Most importantly for this book, we run programmes to do with our relationship with food, alcohol and exercise. Typically, these programmes are subconscious: they are so ingrained in us that we do things through habit and often without giving them any thought at all.

We begin to programme our brains as soon as we are born and most of our programmes are established during our formative years. Beliefs we develop about ourselves and what is important to us drive our programming, thereby determining how we act. The eating habits we develop may stem from emotional issues from the past. For example, a child who felt unloved by his or her parents or who was bullied at school may grow up to seek solace in food, without necessarily realising that this is the case. Others may have grown up feeling unattractive or lonely and turn to food as adults to make themselves feel better. For many, though, they may simply believe that they will always be heavy or don't devote enough time or energy to themselves, stopping them from treating their bodies with the respect they deserve.

Whatever the case for you, until the subconscious triggers for your bad eating habits can be successfully identified and replaced with new, empowering programmes, your weight will either stay on or will pile back on later. In *Lose Weight with NLP* I'll show you how to remove any negative programming for good.

How NLP will work for you

This book will help you to understand the relationship between your brain, the language you use and the habits you have developed, and will give you the necessary tools to change them to help you achieve your weight-loss goals.

You will learn how to use NLP to:

- Create a vision of what you want for yourself for the future
- Take control of your thoughts and language
- Understand your personal beliefs about food and change the ones that are negative
- Let go of negative beliefs about yourself that may be holding you back
- Become aware that you owe it to yourself to be healthy
- Banish cravings for ever
- Enjoy your new, healthier eating and drinking habits
- Find the motivation to exercise
- Shed those pounds once and for all

If I were to sum up NLP in a sentence I'd describe it as an instruction manual for the mind, enabling us to discover what is currently going on in our heads, keeping what works and changing what doesn't! I guarantee that if you are prepared to invest the time and energy into mastering the NLP techniques in this book, your weight-loss battle will finally be over and your life will never be the same again.

Stop Dieting and Start Living!

Here is an important piece of news: diets don't work. So whatever diet you are on right now, STOP! This book is *not* a new diet fad. It is a way to lose weight that is enjoyable and fun and will change your life for ever.

Most books about dieting are only about restricting your intake of food in some way. Many of you have probably encountered this type of book before, the type that promises to give you a body to die for and then underdelivers. The problem with these books is that they don't address the most important element of weight loss, the element that will help you lose weight and keep it off.

Here's the secret: the process of *permanent* weight loss starts with how you think and feel about yourself. Many people overeat if they feel sad or stressed, while others live on junk food as they can't be bothered to put more thought into their meals. So going on a crash diet may cause you to lose the pounds for a while, but if you don't change your fundamental attitude towards food and introduce good eating habits, then the weight just piles back on.

Why restrictive diets don't work

Staggeringly, the number of obese people has increased by almost 400 per cent in the last 25 years and obesity will soon pass smoking as the number-one cause of premature death in the UK. And, due to obesity, it's anticipated that for the first time in over 100 years today's generation of children will have a shorter life-expectancy than that of their parents. The UK is also the country with the third highest obesity rate in the world, behind the US and Mexico. At the same time, the media bombards us with images of thin and attractive young people, airbrushed to glossy perfection, with the subliminal message that we too could look like that if only we were slim. So it's not surprising that so many people turn to the latest fad diet in an attempt to shed some of those extra pounds.

If you've picked up this book, it's likely that you've been on a diet in the past. Maybe you've been on many. According to Marilyn Glenville, author of *Fat Around the Middle*, up to a third of women become as much as a stone heavier once they stop dieting and go back to eating how they did before they restricted food. This can promote a cycle of losing weight and regaining it time and time again – yo-yo dieting in other words. So why are there so many diet books or products that promise you a quick fix? The diet industry is big business and they want you to fail. If all the diet products out there worked in the way that they say they do, we'd live in a thin society and the manufacturers would go out of business. This is clearly not the case, so something else must be going on.

One way that the diet industry sets us up for failure is to create unrealistic expectations. You cannot physically lose more than two pounds of fat a week. This is because to lose one pound you need to achieve a calorie deficit of 3,500 by eating less and exercising more. So this means that a magazine with the headline 'Lose 7 pounds in 7 days' is simply lying as you'd need to create a calorie deficit of 24,500 calories over the week, which equates to burning 4,000 calories a day. To put this into perspective, someone weighing 12 stone would have to run just under 38 miles a day to achieve that sort of result. That's the equivalent of almost one and a half marathons! And that's *before* the calorific content of food is taken into account.

A severe restriction of food is not natural for the body. Without nutrients your body does not have the fuel to do what it needs to do. When you lose weight quickly a quarter of that weight loss will be water, muscle and bone – not the fat you want to lose. Marilyn says that your body 'goes into survival mode, holding on to the weight you have, slowing your metabolism and telling you to eat, eat, eat.' So when you return to your normal diet, your metabolism is slower than before and you end up putting on more weight, and your body will have learned to store fat in case another 'famine' is imminent.

Why are we getting fatter?

There are many reasons for rising obesity levels. First of all, as our lives have become increasingly hectic, stress levels are higher than ever, meaning that many of us are living with our bodies constantly experiencing the 'fight or flight' response. When this happens, it causes your body to shut down your digestion and release the stress hormone cortisol. Once you calm down again the cortisol tells your body it is hungry in order to give you enough energy to be prepared for the next stressful situation. This means that people under continual stress will be tempted to eat more often than they need to and are much more likely to store excess fat, particularly around the middle.

We are also increasingly turning to alcohol to deal with rising stress levels. Alcohol contains empty calories (i.e. calories that serve no nutritional purpose) and acts as an anti-nutrient, meaning it blocks the good effects of your food. You are also much more likely to overeat under the influence of alcohol, as you are tempted to lose control, while many alcoholic drinks act as liquid carbohydrate so they hit the bloodstream fast and make you lose water and feel dehydrated. The body deals with this as stress and again raises cortisol levels, creating a vicious circle.

Thirdly, our lifestyles have become more sedentary than those of our parents and grandparents, with only a third of men and a quarter of women achieving the Department of

Health's target of 30 minutes of exercise five times a week. With more cars on the road than ever before and gadgets that now do the simplest of tasks for us, it's no wonder we're all gaining weight, while our children are becoming the worst offenders of all, sitting around spending most of their free time using social media, computer games or iPhone apps.

Finally, how and what we eat is also having a huge impact on our weight. Food on the go has become the norm for many of us, with one in four British workers not taking a full lunch hour and many skipping lunch altogether, placing an unnecessary strain on the digestive system. Our bodies are designed to survive best on natural, unprocessed food, but the modern diet is loaded with refined carbohydrates, sugar and processed foods full of artificial preservatives and colourings. And with more and more fast-food options becoming available, it's easier than ever before to avoid making our meals from scratch and to live on a diet seriously lacking in essential nutrients.

Sounds scary, doesn't it? However, there are many quick and easy changes you can make to your eating habits, diet and lifestyle and I'll tell you what they are. But before we get to that stage it's essential that you discover your own eating patterns and which bad habits your attitude towards food is causing you to adopt, so that's what we'll do now.

What sort of eater are you?

On any journey of change it's good to know where you've travelled from to enable you to measure your success more easily. Below you'll find a food diary, which I suggest you keep for one week. The diary should be used to record *everything* you eat and drink over seven days. The point of this exercise is to assess your current eating habits, good and bad, to find out if you're giving your body the nutrients it needs. You may be surprised by what you learn.

EXERCISE 1: *How well are you eating?*

When you complete this exercise, it is really important to be totally honest with yourself. It's easy to 'forget' to add that bar of chocolate, second glass of wine or mound of sticky toffee pudding. However, you are only fooling yourself and sabotaging your chances of success if you don't list everything that passes your lips – alcoholic drinks and water included. Be as specific as you can, e.g. large/small glass of wine, two dessertspoons of broccoli, etc. You should also make a note of the time you eat or drink anything and how you are feeling at that moment. That will enable you to pick out trends and emotional patterns. For example, you might notice that you eat at 10 p.m. each night when you're tired and bored. So, here goes!

Stop Dieting and Start Living!

	Breakfast	Mid-morning	Lunch	Mid-afternoon	Dinner	Snacks
DAY 1						
Time						
Feelings						
DAY 2						
Time						
Feelings						

Lose Weight with NLP

	Breakfast	Mid-morning	Lunch	Mid-afternoon	Dinner	Snacks
DAY 3						
Time						
Feelings						
DAY 4						
Time						
Feelings						

Stop Dieting and Start Living!

	Breakfast	Mid-morning	Lunch	Mid-afternoon	Dinner	Snacks
DAY 5						
Time						
Feelings						
DAY 6						
Time						
Feelings						

	Breakfast	Mid-morning	Lunch	Mid-afternoon	Dinner	Snacks
DAY 7						
Time						
Feelings						

What did you find out about your eating habits? Make a note of anything that surprised you. Maybe you drink more alcohol than you thought or have now discovered exactly where those snacks keep disappearing to! Is there a particular time of the day when you binge-eat for comfort? Maybe you eat far more takeaways or processed food than you expected. Whatever conclusions you have drawn, make a note of them here:

Conclusions

_____

_____

_____

_____

_____

EXERCISE 2: *Your vital statistics*

You may not be thrilled about this and yet it's important to make a note of your vital statistics as a starting point for this programme. If you don't, you won't know exactly how well you are doing. And what could give you a bigger boost than knowing you've lost two inches off your hips! So let's measure your weight, body mass index and hip-to-waist ratio.

Step 1: Your weight

Your scales tell you your weight in either stones and pounds or kilos. But it is what those pounds are made up of that defines how lean you are. You could have very little fat on your body but weigh quite a lot due to the amount of muscle you have. So your actual weight is limited as a measure and yet it's what we most often pay attention to which is why we are recording it here. When embarking on this new healthy-eating plan, my suggestion is that you pay more attention to how loose your clothes are becoming, stepping on the scales only once a week at most.

My weight is (in stones or kilos): _____

Step 2: Your BMI

Your body mass index or BMI is a rough estimation of your body's composition and is measured by comparing your weight with your height. However, the drawback is that the BMI measure does not allow for variations in fat, bone, organs and muscle. In other words, the BMI of an extremely fit and muscular person may be the same as an unfit and fat person's simply because their height and weight are the same. It's still something that's worth finding out, though, as it is used widely as a way of determining whether a person is overweight or not.

You can work out your BMI by dividing your weight in kilograms by the square of your height in metres. For example, if your weight is 70 kg and your height is 1.80 m, your BMI will be 70 divided by 1.80 squared (i.e. 70 ÷ (1.80 x 1.80) = 21.60). The clinical definition of being over-weight is having a body mass index, or BMI, of 25 or more; obesity is defined as having a BMI of 30 or higher; and morbid obesity is when your BMI is 40 or above.

My BMI is: _____

Step 3: Your hip-to-waist ratio

This is found by measuring, in centimetres, your waist at its narrowest point and your hips at their widest point. Divide your waist measurement by your hip measurement and that will give you your hip-to-waist ratio. For example, if your waist measures 80 cm and your hips are 101 cm, divide 80 by 101 and you will have a hip-to-waist ratio of 0.79. For women, a result of 0.9 or more means you are on dangerous ground, while for men it's 0.95 or above.

*My hip-to-waist ratio is:*_____

Hopefully, that wasn't too traumatic! The measurements you've taken will act as your starting point for the programme and will make it easy for you to see how well you are doing as you progress through it.

EXERCISE 3: *Your eating style*

Over the years of working with people to help them lose weight, I've noticed the same eating patterns occurring with them time and time again. Take the following test to discover which style of eater you are. We will then explore later in the book why you have adopted those habits and I'll give you techniques to change them once and for all, helping you to lose, and keep off, that excess weight.

Step 1: Score each statement as follows in the shaded box: 1 = strongly disagree, 2 = disagree, 3 = neutral, 4 = agree, 5 = strongly agree.

	Emotional Eater (EE)	Big Eater (BE)	People Pleaser (PP)	Addictive Eater (AE)	Lazy Eater (LE)	Control-Freak Eater (CFE)
I often snack late at night	1					
I rarely leave anything on my plate		2				
I don't like to refuse anything my partner or others cook for me			5			
I think about food all day long				5		
I eat more than one takeaway each week					1	
Food helps me feel in control of my world						1
When I feel stressed I eat more	4					
I go to restaurants where I know I'll get a decent portion		1				
I eat more when I'm in a relationship			1			
I eat so fast I can't really taste my food				1		
I hate food shopping					1	
Food is the only way I feel I can express myself						1
I eat more when I'm lonely	4					

Stop Dieting and Start Living!

	Emotional Eater (EE)	Big Eater (BE)	People Pleaser (PP)	Addictive Eater (AE)	Lazy Eater (LE)	Control-Freak Eater (CFE)
I often finish off other people's meal's		1				
My partner doesn't understand what I like to eat most			1			
I regularly crave sugary snacks				1		
I regard food as fuel					1	
I use the way I eat to get a reaction from those around me						1
I often regret what I've eaten as soon as I've eaten it	1					
I enjoy restaurants where you can eat as much as you like		1				
My partner is putting on weight and so am I			1			
I can't save snacks for later or another day				1		
I always have a supply of ready meals at home					4	
I have a routine regarding food that I like to stick to						2
I eat when I feel under pressure	4					
I enjoy feeling stuffed		1				
I don't like to think of my partner or friends eating alone so I join in			1			
There are foods that I can't stop eating once I start				4		

	Emotional Eater (EE)	Big Eater (BE)	People Pleaser (PP)	Addictive Eater (AE)	Lazy Eater (LE)	Control-Freak Eater (CFE)
I rarely cook anything that takes longer than 10 minutes					1	
I get stressed if I can't stick to my routine regarding food						2
Eating gives me pleasure	4					
I rarely say 'no' when food is being dished onto my plate		2				
I often go along with what others are eating			4			
I often feel out of control with my eating				1		
I often don't have the 'right' foods to eat in my fridge					1	
I can be secretive about the food I eat						1
Totals:	18	8	13	13	9	8

Once you've answered all the questions, add your scores together, working vertically, and write down your total score for each column.

Step 2: Interpreting your results

Now write down what you scored for each eating style:

Emotional Eater (EE):

Big Eater (BE):

People Pleaser (PP):

Addictive Eater (AE):

Lazy Eater (LE):

Control-Freak Eater (CFE):

You should first note the eating style against which you scored highest. This is the style that is most influential in your life, at least at this point in time. A score of 24–30 is very high, 18–23 is moderately high, 12–17 is mid-range to low, and anything below 12 is very low. Then take a look at your second-highest score, as this eating style is also likely to play a large role in determining your eating habits. If you had two highest scores that are the same, that's fine – it just means that your eating habits can vary according to different reasons in your life right now. This is not unusual, for example there is a connection between Addictive and Emotional Eaters.

Interpreting your eating style

Here are the descriptions of each eating style. Read the ones you scored highest against particularly closely to see how well they describe your current relationship with food.

Emotional Eater

The EE uses food to compensate for something that is lacking in their life. For example, they might turn to food to stifle feelings of boredom, loneliness or stress. The EE uses food to change a negative mood and to deal with their emotions. Examples of Emotional Eaters are those people who feel they are unattractive and so eat to drown their sorrows, or those who decide that they can eat exactly what they like as they've had a bad day at work. However, the satisfaction is normally short-lived and can be followed by feelings of guilt, which can spark off another bout of emotional eating.

Katherine – an Emotional Eater

Katherine is one of my control-group clients. She is 38, six foot tall and began the project at 13.5 stone. She had been yo-yo dieting all her life and her goal is to get back to 11 stone. She is an Emotional Eater. Her family used food regularly as a reward and she had been conditioned to believe that she deserved food treats after working hard. She used to overeat, especially when tired and lonely.

Kath has adopted the eating and drinking habits recommended in this book and now feels much more in control of her food choices. She eats little and often and has adopted the 80/20 rule so she still has the occasional treat. She has been drinking much more water and now plans ahead so she always has the 'right' kind of food in the house. She realised that she had been focusing on what she didn't want – being fat – and her Vision Board (see chapter 3, exercise 4) has enabled her to focus on her goals in a much more positive way. She visualises herself at her target weight each day and goes to the gym regularly. She has started to use the services of a personal trainer to help keep her on track. She worked on changing her old belief from 'I'm not in control of what I eat' to 'I am in control of what I eat and am a fit, healthy and slim person'.

In the three months since I started working with Kath, she has lost 15 pounds, and many of her friends, family and colleagues have been remarking on her new shape and vitality. She is full of energy and enjoys investing time and energy in herself.

Big Eater

The BE doesn't like waste. They may have been made to eat everything on their plate as a child. They often clear their plates, even if they are way past feeling full, and may even clear the plates of others, especially their children. They also enjoy getting value for money from their food – quantity can be more important than quality. For example, a carvery may be chosen over an à la carte menu.

People Pleaser

The PP likes to keep everyone happy and they hate to say 'no' to others, leading them to putting other people's needs before their own. They will eat food that they know isn't good for them because someone else has prepared it and they don't want to hurt their feelings. They feel bad at the thought of telling someone that they would prefer to eat something else.

Addictive Eater

The AE craves junk food, refined carbohydrates, sugary snacks and fizzy drinks because they are addicted to the chemical composition of these foods. They have great difficulty in resisting these types of foods or stopping eating them once they have started. They think about food a lot of the time and display a lack of control around it. They are people of extremes who may also be likely to give up their 'normal' eating habits if they feel guilty about a heavy eating period, and are the type of eater most susceptible to trying faddy diets. This feast-or-famine attitude is not good for the body.

Lazy Eater

For the LE, food is low on their list of priorities. They see food purely as 'fuel', i.e. something they have to do to keep going, and can't be bothered to plan or prepare meals. They may not overeat but often opt for ready meals and take-aways, causing them to consume excess calories and too few nutrients. Sometimes they even forget to eat then binge later on the 'wrong' foods.

Control-Freak Eater

The CFE is terrified of feeling out of control in their world. They often use food as a way of controlling what they can – especially if they believe that other areas of their life, such as work, relationships with significant others, etc., are out of control. They tend to turn to food when things begin to feel unmanageable, when ridiculous expectations are put upon them by others, for example, or they can't express themselves in the way they want.

Were you surprised by what you learned about yourself in this chapter? I wonder if you came out as the type of eater you expected. When I was testing out the process I gave the questionnaire to an overweight friend to complete and she was surprised that she came out as a Big Eater. Then on reflection she remembered that at an early age she wasn't allowed to leave the table until her plate was cleared, and she realised that this habit had followed her into adulthood. Just imagine the consequences over a lifetime if your subconscious mind has been trained to clear every plate of food you eat – sometimes not only your own! In the next chapter we'll delve more deeply into why you are the style of eater you are. That's when you can begin making changes to these habits and start to discover a new you.

Defining the New You

By writing down your current vital statistics, you have already set a starting point for your weight-loss journey. Now we're going to develop a vision or goal of where you want to end up. Maybe you're wondering why you should bother with goals? You have probably set goals in your life that you have achieved, and many more that you have not. What made the difference? This would have depended entirely on whether or not you believed these objectives were within your reach. NLP will make your goals achievable by helping you to realise that anything you set your mind to is possible.

So, why is having a goal so important?

- Goals provide motivation, persistence and desire
- Goals help you to concentrate your time and effort
- Goals help you to establish priorities
- Goals take you from where you are to where you want to be

EXERCISE 4: *The journey begins*

Step 1: Discovering what you want

Imagine yourself in a year's time. A year might sound like a long time, but this book is not about going on a crash diet.

We learned why those don't work in Chapter 2. Losing weight with NLP is less about restricting what you eat and more about a healthy lifestyle plan that will last a lifetime. What do you want to have achieved within that year? Aim for a goal that stretches you and is realistic at the same time. Remember that a healthy weight loss of 2 lbs per week for a year would be a maximum weight loss of 104 lbs (7 stone 4 lbs) or 47.17 kg. Of course, if you just want to shed a few pounds after Christmas or after a baby, your desired weight loss will clearly be far less than that! Picture yourself having achieved your goal, then imagine what you'll see, hear and feel.

Consider:

- *What weight do you want to be?* Be very specific about this, i.e. to the exact stone and pound or kilo.

- *What will you look like?* Again, get very specific on this. For example, 'I'll be wearing size 16 clothes' or 'I'll fit into size 10 trousers'. What will you see when you look in the mirror?

- *What will you hear others saying about you? What will you be saying to yourself?* Consider the exact words your friends and family will say to congratulate you.

- *How will you be feeling?* For example, as well as feeling proud of your achievement you may also notice how much easier it is to walk up the stairs or you may feel that you have lots more energy to be able to make the most of each day.

Now turn up the brightness and size of the image, increase the sounds and ramp up the feelings. It may help to close your eyes. Make sure that you are looking through your own eyes and not seeing yourself in the picture.

Keep this image clear in your mind as you move on to the next stage: developing your Vision Board.

Step 2: Creating a new you

Now the fun starts. One of the first things I learned as a new practitioner of neuro-linguistic programming is that a goal must be more than just words on a piece of paper. The exercise you have just completed was the warm-up and will have given you lots of ideas about where you want to be in a year. Now you are going to bring those images to life.

The way to do this is by creating a Vision Board of what you want. You'll need some materials for this exercise, such as some colourful magazines with photographs that represent your goal. For example, you may look for photos of places you want to travel to and activities you can easily do once you have lost weight and have more energy. One of my control group has a photo of herself in a stylish black cocktail dress; another wants to go on a sailing holiday but has been too heavy so he has a photo of a yacht; another has been unable to walk very far without getting breathless so she has pictures of the Lake District on her board, which is where she aims to go on a walking holiday. Get the idea?

Then find photos that represent what you want to look like in a year. Get hold of some felt-tip pens, glue, scissors, a sheet of flip-chart-sized paper (if possible, though any size will do) and anything else you'd like to use. Now, create some space where you can spread out all your materials. Add quotes and phrases that you find inspirational, any motivational messages to yourself and perhaps a photo of you when you were previously at your ideal weight. Allow yourself to go for it and have fun, adding anything that inspires you. When your Vision Board is complete, find a way of displaying it so you can see it easily. I buy clip frames, which protect the board and make it easy to hang on the wall. (You can get them from places like Hobbycraft, Habitat or IKEA.)

Once you have finished your Vision Board, it is very important not just to look at it but also to step into the feelings you will experience once your goals are achieved. This part of the process is crucial to its success. You do this by really putting yourself into all of the experiences you have selected – as a participant not a bystander. For example, using the experiences above, you would imagine wearing the new black cocktail dress, seeing yourself in the mirror and noticing how good that feels. Or you would be on the yacht feeling the warmth of the sun on your back, having fun and so on.

Step 3: Questions for success

The next stage of the process involves you reinforcing all the work you've done so far by asking yourself the questions below. (These questions are adapted from 'Keys to an Achievable Outcome' found in *Time Line Therapy and the Basis of Personality* by Tad James and Wyatt Woodsmall.) It is very important to write the answers down because once you commit the details of your goal to paper, the goal itself begins to feel much more real. Answering these questions will also help you to check that you know *exactly* what you're aiming for, that you're motivated enough to achieve it, that you have everything you need to achieve it and, most importantly, that it is realistic.

So here goes . . .

1 *What specifically do you want?*

_____

_____

_____

2 *For what purpose do you want this goal?*

_____

_____

_____

3 *Where are you now in relation to your goal?*

_____

_____

_____

4 *How will you know when you have achieved your goal?*

_____

_____

_____

5 *What do you have now and what do you still need to achieve your outcome?*

_____

_____

_____

6 *Do you know anyone who has done something similar?*

_____

_____

_____

7 *What will you gain or lose when you achieve your goal?*

_____

_____

_____

8 *What's your level of commitment from 1–10 to achieving this goal? (1 = low and 10 = high)*

_____

_____

_____

What did you notice happening to your goal as you went through that process? I'm sure you will have found that it became much clearer and you will now feel more committed to achieving it.

Let's reflect on a few of the questions and some of the issues they may have highlighted. Number 2 is important because if you just think losing weight is something you *should* do but aren't desperate to do, or if you're only doing it because someone else has told you you should, you will not be motivated to take the action necessary to reach your goal.

Question number 7 is very interesting as it flushes out what is called 'Secondary Gain' in NLP. It asks you to think about what you will lose as well as gain when you get your goal. For example, if becoming fit and healthy means you will need to stop eating certain foods and drinking less alcohol, that is a loss. If the perceived 'loss' of these things is more important to you than the perceived gain of achieving your goal, you are also likely to end up compromising or even sabotaging your own success. That's why it's so important to have an amazing goal that will keep you going even when temptations are put in your way.

Question 8 is also key because if you haven't rated your level of commitment to achieving your goal as 8 or above, forget it! Come back when the pain of not changing finally triggers you into taking action.

Julian – small lifestyle changes add up to big results

Julian is one of my control-group clients. He is 58 and weighed 16 stone at the start of the project. He wanted to separate weight from fitness and focus on fitness so he chose not to weigh himself while on the project, with his biggest wish being for his trousers to fit more easily and to have more energy to enjoy life.

Julian is a Lazy Eater, and he believed that he didn't have the body he wanted because he was sedentary for most of his day and enjoyed stodgy foods, which he was brought up on. Until we started working together, food for Julian had always been something he had to do – he just got it over with. He lives on his own and so couldn't be bothered to cook for himself. He also had another downfall – his sweet tooth meant that he regularly indulged in late-night sugary snacks.

The first thing I did was ask Julian to fill out a food diary, which made him realise that he eats less if he is busy and that water helps to manage his hunger. He has taken several key steps with regard to his diet: he has reduced his portion size, cut out bread, stopped eating carbs after 4 p.m. and no longer eats potatoes with meat. He has taken steps to be far more organised with regard to food so he has healthy foods at home and the sugary late-night snacks have been replaced by fruit. He has also stopped drinking fizzy drinks and cut back on wine. On his Vision Board he has an image of a martial arts expert who is very agile and full of energy, as he finds this highly motivating. He now goes to the gym three to four times a week and it's become an integral part of his life – his motivation is embedded into his daily routine.

He has a rule that he follows, though, which he finds makes it more realistic to keep up his new exercise regime as it fits in well with his lifestyle: no more than two consecutive days at the gym and no more than two days without going. He watches movies on his iPhone while at the gym which makes the whole experience more enjoyable.

Willpower was Julian's biggest issue to overcome, so having a clear picture in his mind as to what he is aiming for is very important to him. He uses his Vision Board every day to make sure he constantly remains focused on his goal. He can now see his toes again and three separate friends have told him that he looks younger. He is trimmer, toned and has lost his jowl. He feels much more energised and is enjoying more agility and flexibility in the way that he moves. He is looking better in his clothes and is wearing more modern styles on his slimmer body.

Your moment of truth

Now is your MOMENT OF TRUTH as it's time to begin taking action. You've worked on your goals and all that's left to do is to really go for it. When you make a decision to change your future, there will always be consequences. Some of these you will be aware of, some not. It's impossible to plan for every eventuality. You have to jump off the edge of the cliff, have faith and learn as you fly.

I assess my clients not by what they say but by what they do as that is the true measure of their commitment to personal change. You can talk as much as you like about changing, but if you take no action, everything will stay the same. It's amazing how many people come to me wanting to lose weight and are prepared to change anything except what they eat! It's *you* who must take responsibility for making the changes you want.

One of the important foundations of NLP is the belief that 'Anything less than 100 per cent is sabotage.' If you're not 100 per cent committed to your goal, you will lose motivation at some point on your journey. So apply the techniques in this book, be willing to be flexible in your approach and, most importantly, be prepared to do WHATEVER IT TAKES to reach your goal.

Are you ready to get started?

TIP: *If you are still in any doubt as to whether you're committed enough to your goal, ask yourself the question 'What will it cost me if I don't make these changes now?' Turn the clock forward and see a picture of yourself in a year's time even heavier and even more unfit. Ask yourself what impact that will have on your self-esteem, love life, career, ability to get about, etc. How do you feel then? This will give you all the extra motivation you need to do everything in your power to achieve your goal.*

Understanding Your Emotions

As we have already learned, there are many reasons why people put on weight, from giving into cravings caused by fluctuating blood sugar to binge eating after a stressful day at work. However, there are also many people who experience weight issues as a result of more deep-seated emotional problems. Of course, if you only want to lose a few pounds after overindulging at Christmas, for example, or know that the sole reason for your weight gain is lazy eating habits, feel free to skip this chapter. However, if you decide to read on anyway, you may be surprised to discover that something from your past that you maybe haven't ever given much thought to is preventing you from achieving your weight-loss goals time and time again.

If you suspect that you *do* have some unresolved emotional issues that are sabotaging your desire to lose weight, this chapter will help you to discover what we refer to in NLP as your 'personal rule book' with regard to food and alcohol and enable you to begin to move on to a new you. The information and exercises in this chapter are not a replacement for professional assistance; if you feel that you require further guidance, please seek professional help. What

I can promise you, though, is that you'll be surprised at just how much of an impact your belief system will be having on your attempts at losing weight. Curious? Good, so let's get started.

Where do our rules come from?

We are what we eat. We are also what we think and believe. Henry Ford once said, 'Whether you believe you can or you can't, you're right.' You can think of beliefs as an on/off switch in your brain. So if you believe you can't lose weight you won't, and if you believe you can you will. And if you were to gather together all the beliefs you hold to be true about yourself, other people and the world around you, they would make up your personal rule book.

The most important thing for you to realise once and for all is that these beliefs are *not* based on fact. Most of our beliefs are formed at a very young age, normally between birth and the age of seven. We collect our beliefs from those closest to us at that time, such as parents, teachers, religious leaders, close family and any other important people in our lives. Most of us do not consciously decide what we believe and once we have a belief we forget that it can be changed and it becomes our reality. Now, that's very scary.

Yet there are ways in which you can overturn any negative beliefs you have, no matter how long you've had them, and turn them into positive, empowering ones that will ultimately help you to achieve your goals. That's exactly what I'm going to show you how to do in this chapter.

June – eating to feel better

June is now 35, but her childhood had been littered with people close to her who had 'left' her. First of all it was her father when she was two, then her mother died when she was ten and her grandmother died when she was fifteen. She believed that she wasn't worthy enough of being loved and that that was the reason everyone had left her.

As she grew into adulthood, she began to eat when she felt lonely. The urge to eat was biggest at night after work and at the weekends. When she felt lonely she would binge on sugary foods such as chocolate, biscuits and alcohol. During the day she could control it more as she was around people at work who kept her mind off food. However, as soon as she got home she would feel a pressure to start to eat. She would imagine how good it would be to eat all her favourite foods. She felt better as she was eating, but as soon as she stopped she began to feel guilty. This guilt would then make her feel even worse about herself, which would encourage her to eat more. She was trapped in a vicious circle.

Using the exercises in this book, we worked together on her limiting beliefs about herself, especially the belief that she was not loveable. She was initially shocked to discover that there was a connection between feeling lonely and unloved and her eating habits. Just helping her make that connection meant that she could start to change her attitude towards herself, which in time helped to improve her self-esteem and enabled her to realise that she is indeed loveable. The positive way she now saw herself then made it easier for her to make new friends and get out more, and she was able to break the vicious circle of eating to feel better.

EXERCISE 5: *My personal myths*

Step 1: Your personal myths are your beliefs about your current weight. We are interested here in the negative ones that are likely to have led you to becoming overweight and then kept you stuck. Here are some examples:

- I don't deserve to lose weight
- My metabolism is too slow
- Diets don't work for me
- Everyone in my family is overweight so it's inevitable I will be too

- It gets much harder to lose weight during mid-life and later

- I'm big-boned

- I can't lose weight, no matter what I do

- Being fat is in my genes

- It's too expensive to eat healthily

List your personal myths below:

_____

_____

_____

_____

_____

_____

_____

Step 2: This time we're going to flush out what I call 'food viruses' by filling in the rest of the sentence 'I don't have the body I want yet because . . .' Here you might come up with food viruses like:

- I'm too lazy

- I'm useless at the gym

- I'm rubbish at everything I do

- I enjoy the wrong foods

- I drink too much

- I hate exercise

- I've got no willpower

- I'm easily led by others

List your food viruses below:

_____

_____

_____

_____

_____

_____

_____

Step 3: What did you learn about yourself from those two steps? Use the space below to write this down.

_____

_____

_____

_____

_____

_____

When you read back over your myths and viruses, things that you believe to be true, notice how they now appear to be simply excuses that are holding you back from becoming the person you want to be. Just imagine for a moment if none of these statements were true for you. What difference would that make to your aim to become healthier? That's right – there would be nothing in your way to stop you. Well, I've got news for you – none of your personal myths or your food viruses are true! And now I'm going to show you how to identify events or situations from your past that may have led to these negative beliefs. Once these have been removed, the next chapter will then help you to reprogramme your brain so you can let go of all these excuses and take responsibility for what you want in your life.

Letting go of negative experiences from the past

Now, this section involves a certain amount of soul searching. You may have already been well aware of some of your myths and viruses as they are perhaps things you tell yourself on a regular basis or when you realise that you've failed in yet another attempt to lose weight. However, if you don't delve deeper into your emotions until you find exactly what it is that has triggered these myths and viruses, you will never succeed in achieving what you want for yourself.

I've worked with many people aiming to lose weight and some of the situations that have held back my clients have included the following:

- They were teased or bullied at school
- They frequently changed school and/or house
- They had struggled to deal with their parents' divorce
- They were told they were a failure or not good enough by parents or teachers
- They were told they were unattractive or even ugly
- They suffered emotional or physical abuse

These are just some examples of situations that may be resonating with you now, years after they happened, and are still affecting your ability to lose weight. Your trigger may also be completely different from those listed above, but whatever it is, the important thing is to find the connection between the past and why you eat excessively in the present.

EXERCISE 6: *What's your story?*

Refer back to your eating style questionnaire in Chapter 2 and the previous exercise about personal myths and viruses for clues and tips-offs. Then ask yourself the following questions:

What negative experiences in your past may have led to your weight issues today?

_____

_____

_____

_____

_____

_____

What negative beliefs about yourself have those experiences generated in you?

_____

_____

_____

_____

_____

_____

How have those beliefs acted as a trigger for your weight issues today?

_____

_____

_____

_____

_____

_____

Make a note of the key things you have learned from these questions below:

_____

_____

_____

_____

_____

_____

Changing our stories

Believe it or not, you can actually change your past. Whatever happened, good or bad, you can turn your past on its head by changing your perception of particular events. The following exercise is going to show you how to take steps to change your programming from the past.

The first step involves you becoming aware of the negative experiences from your past that are holding you back, and you did this in the previous exercise. This has brought the issue from a subconscious to a conscious level of understanding. Now I'm going to give you two methods for changing how you feel about those negative experiences.

EXERCISE 7: *Changing your personal history (part 1)*
(*Not to be used for extreme trauma, phobia or abuse*)
This exercise is brilliant for changing a single negative event in the past.

Step 1: Think about the event in the past that you now know is still affecting you today. Step back into the feelings you felt then for a moment. Write down those feelings below:

_____

_____

_____

_____

_____

_____

Step 2: Ask yourself what positive emotional states you needed but didn't have in the past event; states, which, if you'd had then, the event would never have been a problem. For example, if you were bullied you may have needed confidence or courage to deal with it differently. Do your best to think of at least six powerful positive states and write them down here:

_____

_____

_____

_____

_____

_____

_____

Step 3: Now remember specific occasions in the past when you experienced each of these powerful, positive states. For example, times when you felt really confident or courageous. Remember specific times, not just general feelings, e.g. I felt confident on the day I graduated, etc. Write them down below:

Step 4: Taking one specific memory at a time, return to it in your mind. Imagine floating down into your body and looking through your own eyes. See what you saw, hear what you heard and *really* feel the positive feelings you felt at that time. Make the colours brighter, the sounds louder and the feelings even stronger. As you really begin to feel the emotions, apply pressure to the knuckle of your first finger on your left hand with the first finger of your right hand. Continue to apply pressure to the knuckle as you relive the memory through your own eyes. As the pictures, sounds and feelings begin to ebb away, remove your finger from your knuckle. Repeat this for each of your powerful positive

emotions, using the same knuckle each time and 'stacking' these positive feelings on top of one another for maximum effect. In NLP, this is called a Positive Resource Anchor.

Step 5: Next, test out your new resource anchor by pressing your knuckle in exactly the same way (but this time without accessing any specific memory) and notice how differently you feel now. You will feel a combination of all the powerful resourceful states that you stacked. Make sure that this feeling is significantly more intense than the emotions associated with the negative event in the past. If you need it to be even stronger, add some more powerful and positive states until it is stronger than the emotions associated with the past event.

Step 6: Now relive the negative event in the past by imagining you are back there, seeing the situation through your own eyes. As you do this, press your knuckle to fire off your Positive Resource Anchor until all the negativity surrounding the event has disappeared.

Step 7: Test how well this has worked by asking yourself how those events in the past feel differently now. They are still in your memory, of course, but they should now feel totally flat, i.e. the negative emotion should have disappeared. If you are not quite at this stage yet, repeat the process until you are.

EXERCISE 8: *Changing your personal history (part 2)*

This exercise is for those of you who cannot remember a specific event, yet still have some negative emotions or limiting beliefs about yourself from the past.

Step 1: Ask yourself what negative emotion you're feeling, e.g. 'I'm sad' or limiting belief, e.g. 'I'm not good enough'. Write it below:

_____

_____

_____

_____

_____

_____

Step 2: Ask yourself what is it that you need to learn that will allow you to let go of this negative emotion or limiting belief for ever. When you do this, bear in mind that what you write down must be:

- For you
- Positive
- For the future

For example, if you feel that you're not good enough, you might write 'I am good enough. I can be who I want to be. I stopped noticing all the times when I have been good enough and now I can start to notice them again.' If you write 'they didn't know any better', this does not fit the criteria as it's not addressed to you, it's not positive and it's not for the future. Get the idea? Once you turn limiting beliefs about yourself around you will finally be able to let go of events from your past.

Linda – moving on from her past

Linda is one of my control-group clients. She is aged 53, is five foot five and in the last five years has piled on the weight, taking her from 8 stone to 14 stone. Her goal is to get back to 10 stone. She still thinks of herself as a thin person even though she no longer is.

Before she came to me, Linda had been feeling help-less, drinking a bottle of wine a night to mask her feelings, and she hated how she looked and felt. She is an addictive eater and believed that she was out of control and had no willpower. She used to enjoy regular brisk walks but found that her breathlessness was preventing her from being able to go on them any more.

Completing the food diary exercise and logging her feel-ings was a real turning point for her. For the first time, she began to understand why she was overeating and drinking: she realised that it was linked to bereavement. Nearly 20 years ago her mother, grandmother and best friend all died within six weeks of each other. Then five years ago, she lost her father, granddaughter and friend – they all died within six months of each other. She learned that she was using drink to feel relaxed and happy and to get away from the feelings of sadness from her losses. She worked on letting go of the sadness that had been holding her back and began to focus on building her self-esteem.

This has built a much stronger foundation on which she can now lose weight. She has cut out wine in the week and is drinking much more water, which she finds takes away her hunger pangs as well as her need to drink alcohol. Her breathlessness is improving and she can now exercise. She has started walking again and regularly enjoys long walks by the sea. She has cut out white food products, such as white bread, pasta, rice and potatoes, and has reduced her portion size. She's also introduced fish at least twice a week on to the menu. The biggest change is that she is now in control of her eating rather than feeling that food is in control of her, making her feel better about herself. She had a lot of emotional issues from the past to deal with, which she has now done, and she is now ready and motivated to begin seriously to lose weight.

We've worked hard during this chapter to build your awareness of what drives the personal relationship you have with food. People with higher levels of self-esteem have far fewer issues with weight as they feel happier about themselves and their lives, so let's now continue building on the positive image you are developing of yourself by building your self-esteem.

EXERCISE 9: *Building your self-esteem*

Self-esteem flourishes when it receives regular nourishment. This exercise will teach you how to feed your self-esteem to ensure that it continues to grow. It is important that you select only positive qualities as you go through the following steps.

Step 1: Remember a time in the past that you felt really good about yourself. What three qualities did you most admire about yourself back then?

1. _____

_____

2. _____

_____

3. _____

_____

Step 2: What three qualities do you most admire about yourself now?

1. _____

_____

2. _____

_____

3. _____

_____

Step 3: Imagine a time in the future when you have achieved your goals. What three things do you most admire about yourself at that point in time?

1. _____

_____

2. _____

_____

3. _____

_____

Step 4: Think about a person who loves you. What three qualities do they admire most about you?

1. _____

_____

2. _____

_____

3. _____

_____

Step 5: Think about a colleague at work who respects you. What three qualities do you think they admire most about you?

1. _____

_____

2. _____

_____

3. _____

_____

Step 6: Take the 15 words that comprise your answers, write them on a large piece of paper, and hang them somewhere where you can see them every day. Then write them on a smaller piece of paper for you to keep in your handbag or wallet. If you notice yourself drifting back into any negative thoughts about yourself, look back at the piece of paper and remind yourself of all your best qualities.

Natalie – confronting her past and changing her life

Natalie is another of my control-group clients. She is 43 and five foot five and she started the project at 12 stone. Her goal is to get back to her 'normal' weight of 9.5 stone, but she is a Control-Freak Eater and tends to overindulge in food when her mother makes her feel bad. She has always felt that she's a failure in her family as all her siblings and cousins have done better than her financially. She also felt that she didn't have the body she wanted because she didn't deserve it.

The food diary made her aware of the unhealthy patterns of eating she had fallen into and that she ate when bored and unhappy. On her Vision Board she has a photo of a slim, attractive woman in a black dress who is peaceful and calm, and she focuses daily on that picture to keep motivated. She has given up sugary foods at work, especially biscuits, and now she takes fruit to work for the whole office! She has developed an exercise routine that involves going swimming twice a week, going to yoga once a week and walking up to 13 miles at a time at the weekends. She has also stopped drinking alcohol during the week. She has found having a training buddy incred- ibly useful as he has helped her to keep on track by encouraging her to stick to the commitments she makes. So far she has lost 9 pounds and has gone down a clothes size. We have worked together on building her self-esteem, and as a result she has recently signed up to an evening course as she feels she is ready for an exciting career change.

Pulling it all together

This chapter has involved learning about how your past has influenced the issues you have with your weight *now*. You were able to discover your personal beliefs about yourself and how these have been impacting on your attitude towards food and alcohol, keeping you overweight. We also began to link significant emotional experiences from your past to these beliefs and considered how they may have triggered them in the first place. The exercises then showed you how to begin changing your beliefs about your past, thereby changing your thoughts and your feelings in the present. We learned that it's possible to change any belief we have by reprogramming our mind, and we'll now take that further in the next chapter.

TIP: *Many weight problems begin as an emotional issue. Once you can learn and move on from that experience you will find losing weight a much easier process.*

Reprogramming
Your Brain

W e've seen how closely the mind and body are linked. If you think back to a time in your life when you achieved something, I doubt that it was when you felt miserable and depressed! It goes without saying that we get our best results when our minds and bodies are in alignment in supporting us to achieve our goals.

In the last chapter we started to change the negative thoughts and beliefs you have about yourself that influence your weight. This chapter will help you to establish those positive changes once and for all by giving you the tools you need to reprogramme your brain.

Think thin!

S o let me start with the basics first. *You* determine whether or not you are overweight. Everything you have believed up until now – all your personal myths and thought viruses – have brought you to this point. Your body shape can be redefined because everything in your world has been created by *you*. You alone choose your thoughts and decide between what is and isn't possible for you to achieve.

The good news is that redefining your world, and therefore your thoughts, is really one of the easiest things you can learn. I'm going to teach you how to do it in this chapter.

Focus on what you want

If I were to say to you now, 'Whatever you do, do not think about a blueberry muffin', what happens? That's right, you think about a blueberry muffin! In fact, what actually happens is your mind has to focus on the blueberry muffin first in order not to think about it. This is because our minds cannot process a negative. The saying 'be careful of what you wish for' rings true here because if you produce an unhelpful or harmful thought, or, in NLP terms, an internal representation of something you don't want, the risk is that that's exactly what you'll get. One of the most basic psychological rules in life is that you always get more of what you focus on. This is because your energy flows to where your attention goes. So if you focus on not being fat, not eating that muffin, not drinking that extra glass of wine, etc., you are still keeping those things in the forefront of your mind and you will end up getting exactly what you don't want.

Derren Brown demonstrated this very powerfully on TV using an adorable kitten that he had put in a glass container.

A member of the audience, Lauren, was introduced to the kitten and then showed how the glass container was wired up to a box with a large red button on it. She was told that if she pushed the red button, a bolt of electricity would be transmitted to the glass container and the kitten would die. The task was simply not to kill the cat and she was also offered a reward of £500 for not pushing the red button. What we saw next was extraordinary. Just seconds before the clock ran out, Lauren went over to the red button and pushed it, killing the cat! Of course, the kitten wasn't really dead. The point is that when we focus so much on what we want to avoid or what we don't want, ironically that is the very thing we end up getting!

Look back at your personal myths and viruses in the last chapter. You may be surprised to find that you've been sabotaging your efforts at weight loss for years by focusing on exactly what you *don't* want. The key, of course, is to start focusing on what you *do* want, and the next exercise will help you achieve exactly that.

EXERCISE 10: *Reframing your thoughts*

Step 1: List below your personal myths and viruses from the last chapter. In the opposite column write what you would like to focus on instead. For example, 'I don't deserve to lose weight' becomes 'I deserve to lose weight' or 'I can't lose weight as I'm big-boned' becomes 'I have the perfect body for losing weight', and so on. Make sure all the new statements are positive.

Myths / Viruses	What I want to focus on instead

Step 2: Now find somewhere quiet to go with your list of positive statements and focus on these new thoughts. If it makes it easier, say them out loud and repeat until you feel yourself starting to believe what you're saying. If you notice any of the old thoughts creeping back into your mind, make sure you swap them for your new positive ones. Spend at least five minutes each day practising this.

Step 3: Get yourself two jars and a packet of dried peas or similar. Each time you catch yourself thinking one of your new positive thoughts, add one pea to one of the jars. If you find yourself focusing back on one of your old negative thoughts, put a pea in the other jar. Do this over a day and notice which jar has the most peas inside. At the end of the day, empty out the jars and repeat the exercise. Do this each day until you find that the jar with the negative thoughts is empty or very nearly empty. The purpose of this exercise is to make you consciously aware of your subconscious thoughts.

Stay chilled if it takes you quite a while to turn your instinctive thought process into a positive one. If you've been telling yourself something for years, it will obviously take a bit of practice for you to start believing the opposite. The important thing is that you get there in the end as that's when you can start making truly positive changes in your life.

What is your RAS?

Your Reticular Activating System, or RAS, forms a gateway between your conscious and subconscious mind. Think of your conscious mind as your goal setter and your subconscious mind as your goal getter. The goal-setting process is a very logical, conscious process. By contrast, the goal-getting process is something that mostly happens at a subconscious level, with the help of your RAS. Your RAS takes instructions from your conscious mind and passes them on to your subconscious mind, helping you to filter through the data that enters your head to find the bits of information that will deliver to you what you want.

So how will this help you lose weight?

You can deliberately programme this system by choosing the exact messages you send from your conscious mind to your subconscious mind via your RAS. You can do this by focusing on your Vision Board goals. Eighteen months ago, one of my clients started her weight-loss campaign. One of her goals was to run the women-only 5K Race for Life in memory of her father who had died of cancer the year before. She had put on her Vision Board some photos of women previously finishing the race as well as photos of her dad. Before her big day, she went along to one of her local races. While at the race, she enjoyed cheering on the women and watching their elation as they crossed the finish line and afterwards she found a discarded running number that she stuck on her Vision Board. She was then able to feel really motivated about her own goal as she imagined herself successfully crossing that line. She not only saw it in her mind, but also heard the noise of the crowd cheering her on and felt the feelings of success. And, although she was creating the images consciously, she was giving her RAS an image to pass on to her subconscious mind with a note that said, in effect, 'work on this for me, please'.

Your RAS helps you to achieve your goals as it cannot

distinguish between 'real events' and 'imagined' reality. In other words, it tends to believe whatever you focus on to be true for you. Athletes use this technique a lot, effectively rehearsing their sport in their mind before they actually go out and do it. This is what my client was doing by imagining herself successfully completing the race. She was acting as if she had already achieved it. And that is exactly what she went on to do the following year.

This is why when you set your goal you must create a very definite image of it in your conscious mind, with pictures, sounds, feelings, tastes and smells. Your RAS will then pass this on to your subconscious mind, which will help you to achieve the goal. Your RAS then brings to your attention all the relevant information that otherwise may have passed you by unnoticed.

Cause v. Effect

In NLP, the concept of 'cause and effect' is a very powerful tool that has the ability to change any area of your life you apply it to. One of our finest skills as humans is to absolve ourselves of responsibility. When something goes well, we like to take credit for it; when something goes badly, we tend to shift blame. Those people who are successful at weight loss are prepared to take a long hard look at themselves and take responsibility for their situation regardless of how they got

Lose Weight with NLP

there. This is called living life 'at cause'. Once you begin to put yourself at cause and take responsibility for everything in your life, things will stop simply 'happening' to you and you will actively start creating the life you want and deserve.

Living life 'at effect'

Over the years I've found that the idea of taking action and doing something different is what holds most overweight people back. Instead, they search for external fixes. This is called living life 'at effect'. An example of this would be opting for a tummy tuck rather than changing your diet and introducing exercise into your lifestyle.

People who live life at effect do not take responsibility for what happens to them. They tend to blame others when things do not go their way, making excuses for why they cannot do what they should do. Simply waiting and hoping for things to improve or for others to provide for your well-being makes you a victim of your circumstances. Those at effect portray themselves as victims because they believe they have no choices. However, the reality is that they have chosen not to take any responsibility for their actions.

This might sound harsh, yet, as we discovered earlier, if you are overweight you only have yourself to blame. If you hear yourself saying things like 'I can't lose weight because I'm big-boned / it's in my genes / my metabolism isn't working / I'm too old / I've tried dieting and it doesn't work / I'm too stressed / I don't like exercise / I'm too lazy', and so on, you are creating excuses for remaining overweight and living your life at effect. If this applies to you, it's time to start taking responsibility for yourself and regain the control you've lost. It's your life, don't you want to decide want happens to it?

Lucy – taking control of her own body

Lucy was 34, overweight and had dieted many times over the years. The last time she lost over four stone (about 56 lbs, or 25 kg) on the latest fad diet to come out of California. It was fantastic being slim, yet after a while she began to revert to her old habits. In the end it was tragic, as she regained all the weight she'd lost – and more! She came to me distraught and desperate to lose the weight again. In fact, I was her last stop before resorting to a gastric band. I was so glad that she sought my help. Having a gastric band fitted is an example of the ultimate 'effect' behaviour. I told Lucy that having a major operation to shrink the size of her stomach so she could not eat would be like admitting that she had absolutely no control over herself. I worked with her to create a vision of what she wanted, and we planned a new healthy eating and exercise regime, one that was gradual and achievable. We also worked on solving the underlying psychological reasons why she had subconsciously sabotaged her efforts to lose weight in the past. This made all the difference as Lucy discovered that at a subconscious level her weight covered up her very low confidence and self-esteem, so we were able to work together to change her belief patterns about herself. Lucy reached her target weight again and this time she has managed to maintain it. She has permanently changed what she eats and introduced an exercise regime that she enjoys. She loves what she has achieved and relishes being back in control of her life.

Living life 'at cause'

In contrast, those who live their life 'at cause' take personal responsibility for everything that happens to them. People on the cause side are always searching inside for a solution and a way to learn from their mistakes. They know that it is them and them alone who are responsible for their bodies and what they have created – good or bad! This puts them in a position of power over their situation and gives them the ability to make any changes they desire. They use empowering language to support themselves in achieving their goals, such as 'I can', 'I will', 'It's going to be easy', 'I am in control of my life', 'I choose not to eat that doughnut' and so on. The result is that they keep hold of their own personal power in any situation.

It goes without saying that when you move from effect to cause, you feel more empowered and stronger than you ever did before. Much of NLP is effectively designed to put you back at cause. If you want to move from the 'effect' to the 'cause' side of the equation, the first step is to remove all of your excuses. This can be a less-than-comfortable process at first; however, I guarantee that once you begin to get the results you want, you will feel differently.

EXERCISE 11: *Living life 'at cause'*

Answer the following questions in the context of your current weight situation:

How have I managed to create this situation in my life?

_____

_____

_____

_____

_____

What is there for me to learn from this situation?

_____

_____

_____

_____

_____

What do I need to do differently from now on so this never happens again?

_____

_____

_____

_____

_____

Start asking yourself these questions whenever something in your life does not go quite to plan and soon you will notice that you will begin to get different results. When you ask these questions you may notice answers popping into your mind that you didn't expect to get. That's great, because they are bubbling up from your subconscious mind and you should pay attention to whatever you hear. If you fall off the wagon during your new regime, ask yourself these questions as they will ensure that you get back on track again quickly and continue to move towards your goal.

Pulling it all together

Let's reflect back on what it takes to reprogramme your brain. There are certain core elements that are essential for you to remember:

- You are the creator of your own universe: you alone choose your thoughts and decide between what is and what isn't possible for you to achieve

- Your nervous system cannot process negatives: focus on what you want as opposed to what you don't want, otherwise you'll get what you don't want

- Use positive language about what you want to achieve: tell yourself you can and will become who you want to be

- Create clear goals: your RAS needs goals so it can search out the people, information and events that will serve you best

- Live life 'at cause': take responsibility for getting the body you want

- Taking 100 per cent responsibility for the results you want will give you the motivation to keep going until you achieve your goal

TIP: *Remember that all your results start as a thought. You will lose weight if you believe it is possible.*

Your Healthy Lifestyle

This chapter is not meant to be a replacement for professional medical services, nor is it the gospel on health and nutrition. It is a collection of good common sense about eating and drinking that I have gathered over the years. Each one of our bodies is different so please experiment with the information and tips provided here. The key thing for you to remember is that your body is the vehicle through which you experience life. If you put in the time and effort required to nourish your body and keep it at a healthy weight and good level of fitness, it will help you to enjoy life to its full potential.

Of course, to experience the benefits you are aiming for on your Vision Boards, you will have to be active in bringing about these changes. It's time to ditch the excuses and shift over to the cause side of the equation, focusing clearly on the results you want. It's time for you to be prepared to make changes.

This chapter first explores what not to eat, before moving on to what should be included in your new, healthy diet. We'll also explore how to get your metabolism working efficiently, and there are exercises for you to do that will help you change your approach to eating depending on the style of eater you are. Finally, I will guide you in determining what your own goals for a healthy lifestyle should be, and will show you how to commit to them fully to make sure you achieve them.

What not to eat and drink

Although it's hard to believe, food and drink companies want us to get addicted to the wrong foods as it makes them more money! Every day we are brainwashed into eating the wrong foods because of healthy-sounding labels and our own ignorance.

Remember Sunny Delight? Launched in 1998 with a £10 million promotional campaign, within months Sunny Delight had become the biggest-selling soft drink in the UK behind Coke and Pepsi, with sales of £160 million a year. Then it all went terribly wrong.

The Food Commission, an independent consumer organisation, started to question what was actually in Sunny Delight. The healthy attributes that were being claimed by its marketing campaign were not true and it turned out to be a totally artificial product. It was full of oil, colours, chemicals and preservatives. Clever marketing ploys included the close placement of the product next to fresh orange juice in supermarkets and even the shape of the bottle suggested freshly squeezed orange juice.

The moral of this story is to make sure you are always aware of what you're putting into your body and to look beyond the label to the ingredients. Products often highlight the few natural ingredients they contain, even though they also contain many more unnatural or processed things that you only find in the small print of the ingredients list. So it's essential that you start paying much more attention to what you are buying.

So what should we absolutely avoid eating and drinking?

Let's keep this in perspective. I recommend the 80/20 rule. That means that 80 per cent of the time you should eat and drink sensibly, leaving 20 per cent of the time for you to indulge, such as when you're out with friends, it's the weekend or a special occasion. I still eat the occasional dessert and chocolate bar but I do not see them as everyday foods. I remind myself that there's always another time to eat them and I enjoy the fact that I'm in control of my body and my weight. The funny thing is that when you get used to a healthier diet, often these old foods that you used to enjoy start to hold far less appeal for you.

I've grouped the 'dangerous' foods and drinks into the following categories:

- All things white

- Sugary foods

- Junk and processed foods

- Dairy products

- Alcohol

- Caffeine

ALL THINGS WHITE

This means all things made from white flour, including white bread, baguettes, flour tortillas, cakes, biscuits, crackers, pastries and white pasta. These foods are often the biggest culprit in causing people to pile on the pounds.

Our bodies evolved to survive best on natural, unprocessed foods, but the modern diet is loaded with refined foods such as those listed above. It's not just the calories in refined foods that pose a threat to our health, it's also the way they are digested. These foods are quickly turned into sugars in the body, and this causes a rush of insulin into the bloodstream with the purpose of clearing the sugar from your blood before it does any damage. The insulin moves the excess blood sugar from your blood and causes it to be stored as fat, not only on your stomach and hips, but also in your arteries, heart and brain.

You will have felt this process happening in your body before as you get a brief peak of energy as the sugars are released, followed by a bigger slump as the insulin clears out the sugar. As your brain becomes starved of fuel, it tells you that you need to refuel, causing you to become hungry again within a short time. It's a vicious circle. And the insulin produced as your body attempts to clear out the excess sugars causes serious issues all by itself, particularly the risk of type 2 diabetes. Frightening, isn't it?

SUGARY FOODS

This includes cereals, breakfast bars, cakes, biscuits, muffins, pizzas, doughnuts, sweets, ice-cream, chocolate, fizzy drinks, fruit juices (from concentrate), a lot of pre-prepared foods and many takeaway options, especially Chinese food.

JUNK AND PROCESSED FOODS

This means all food from fast-food outlets, snack foods, chips, ready meals, pre-prepared foods such as ready-made pies or chicken nuggets, crisps and margarine.

DAIRY PRODUCTS

This means milk, yoghurt, cream and cheese, and all products made from these foods, such as creamy pasta sauces or cheesecake. Any diet that promotes dairy products is essentially encouraging you to eat and drink growth hormones. The chemical and hormonal structure of milk sets off fast growth in calves and does the same for humans. Do you want to develop like a cow? No, I didn't think so. If you don't want to cut out dairy products, eat only organic varieties as these do not contain growth hormones, antibiotics or pesticides.

The worst foods combine both dairy and wheat products such as pizza, white pasta with a creamy sauce, cereal with milk, cheese sauces, quiche, cheese sandwiches and so on.

ALCOHOL

All alcoholic drinks contain a huge number of calories. These quickly turn into extra pounds because the body metabolises the calories in alcohol before it metabolises fat, meaning that the fat is less likely to be burned off. Alcohol is often described as 'empty calories' as it has no nutritional value other than to provide energy. It can also weaken your willpower, tempting you to eat more than planned, thereby having a double 'whammy' effect. Here are some typical calorific values of wine, beer and spirits:

- Standard glass (175 ml) red wine . . . . . 120 calories

- Standard glass (175 ml) white wine . . . 130 calories

- Pint of bitter . . . . 180–230 calories

- Pint of lager. . . . . 240–250 calories

- Pint of cider. . . . . 180–250 calories

- Gin and tonic . . . . 126 calories

- Gin and low-calorie tonic. . . . . 71 calories

- Dark rum and coke. . . . . 142 calories

- Liqueur (50 ml) . . . . 100–170 calories

- Brandy (50 ml) .... 110 calories
- Whisky (25 ml) .... 55 calories
- Bottle of alcopop .... 160–228 calories

The recommended daily calorie intake is about 2,000 calories for women and 2,500 calories for men, meaning that it's easily possible to drink half of your daily calorie intake in alcohol on a good night out. If this is combined with a meal out or takeaway then you are really in trouble!

CAFFEINE

Reduce your caffeine intake. Coffee, black tea, green tea, chocolate, colas and energy drinks all contain caffeine. Caffeine affects cravings for food because it raises the stress hormone cortisol. In turn, cortisol raises your heart rate and blood pressure and tells your body to increase energy stores – namely carbohydrates and fats. If this happens you'll inevitably gain weight.

Cheap foods will cost you more

Many of my clients tell me that they cannot afford to eat anything other than ready meals and junk food. They believe the myth that it's expensive to eat well. This is simply not true. You can most definitely eat good food on a budget. When was the last time you snacked on a handful of Brazil nuts, a raw carrot or a banana? Brown bread is no more expensive than white, mackerel and sardines are much cheaper than red meat or chicken, and if you buy local fruit and veg that are in season, it's not only cheap, but also contains lots more vitamins and minerals than varieties that have been flown in from far-away destinations.

Junk food may also cost you dearly in other ways, by harming your health and therefore impacting on your enjoyment of life. The hidden costs are enormous – type 2 diabetes, high blood pressure, an increased chance of a stroke . . . the list goes on and on. I've also had clients who get too breathless during a gentle walk and others who are too embarrassed to take their clothes off and enjoy an active sex life. So ask yourself: just how high a cost are you willing to pay with regard to your health and vitality?

What to eat?

You may well be wondering what on earth is left that is healthy for you to eat and drink? Well, the good news is that there is a lot. Genetically, we are almost the same as we were prior to the introduction of grains such as wheat. Cereals, refined carbs and sugar only became part of our diet when agriculture was developed. The foods best suited to our digestive systems are those that were freely available to us at the time we evolved, such as lean animal and fish protein, eggs, nuts, seeds, fruits and vegetables.

What's important here is to ensure that the food you eat is as close to its natural state as possible. Follow the simple rule that if it looks the way it was meant to look, eat it! What's more, it has been proven that organic food often has twice the nutritional value of commercially grown food, so buy the organic versions of these foods as often as possible. I've categorised the healthy foods that should make up the majority of your diet into four groups. Let's take a look at each:

- Creatures from the land
- Creatures from the sea
- Naturally grown foods
- What to drink

CREATURES FROM THE LAND

This means lean meat, poultry and eggs. By the way, it's official: eggs are good for you! An egg is one of the most nutritious food items in our diet as it is rich in protein, vitamins and minerals. Protein foods like lean meat, chicken and eggs help your body to repair tissue, build muscle and grow red blood cells, as well as providing a source of energy and keeping you fuller for longer. Our bodies do not store protein and require a certain amount of it daily, so we need to make sure we include some form of protein at every meal. (Other non-animal forms of protein include tofu, pulses, nuts and seeds.)

CREATURES FROM THE SEA

This encompasses fish and shellfish. Fish is another good source of protein, and it also contains high levels of B vitamins, which are needed for almost every function in the body. Many types of fish are also rich in calcium.

But one of the best types of fish you can eat is oily fish. Salmon, trout, mackerel, herring and sardines are a good source of vitamins A and D, as well as an excellent source of omega-3 fatty acids. (See below for more information on these 'healthy fats'.)

Most shellfish is naturally low in total fat and saturated fat, making it a perfect addition to a heart-healthy diet. Bear in mind, though, that its cholesterol content can be higher than other types of fish so it should be eaten in moderation.

NATURALLY GROWN FOODS

This includes all vegetables, fruits, berries, salad ingredients, beans, seeds and nuts. All nuts have health benefits, such as being high in protein and fibre, and nuts such as walnuts and Brazil nuts are high in omega-3 fatty acids.

We also need to include a wide variety of vitamins and minerals in our diet in order to achieve optimum health, so it's important to eat as many different types of fruits and vegetables as possible. When choosing which fruits and vegetables to eat, it's good to aim for a wide variety of colours.

We need fibre for intestinal health and we get this from dried fruit, including figs, raisins, apricots, dates, etc.; fruits, including avocados, bananas, berries, guava, kiwis, oranges, pears and apples; all pulses, including beans, peas and lentils; and grains such as oats, rye and barley.

Olive oil is rich in monounsaturated fat, a type of fat that researchers are discovering has excellent health benefits as it helps to clean out your arteries as it moves through them.

Soya beans are a good source of protein and can be eaten in their original form or in the form of tofu, soya milk, soya yoghurt or soya cheese. Like omega-3s, soya products also increase your metabolism and encourage weight loss from the stomach area.

Foods that have to be milled and cooked like rice, bread and pasta are not in this category. However, these can be eaten in small amounts but you need to choose the brown varieties, such as wholewheat bread, rye bread, brown rice or wholewheat pasta. For more information on healthy eating visit: www.eatwell.gov.uk/healthydiet/

What to drink

The vast majority of your fluid intake should be made up of water and herbal teas. If you love your tea and coffee, drink decaffeinated varieties. Drink bottled or filtered water regularly throughout the day. Experts recommend that you take your body weight, divide it in half and that is the amount of water fluid in ounces you should be drinking each day. So if you weigh 150 pounds, you should drink 75 fluid ounces of water a day. I keep a two-litre bottle on my desk and take small sips all day long; you may find this helps you as the bottle serves as a reminder to drink more water. If you like to drink milk, there are many good cow's milk alternatives such as organic soya milk, goat's milk, rice milk, almond milk, etc.

Once you have reached your ideal weight, if you do drink alcohol, keep within the recommended limits, i.e. no more than 21 units per week or 3–4 units per day for men and no more than 14 units per week or 2–3 units per day for women. A standard 175 ml glass of wine is approximately one and a half units, while a large glass can be up to 3 units. Depending on the brand's strength, a pint of lager is between 2 and 3 units, while a single 25 ml shot of spirit equates to 1 unit.

And, watch out for fresh fruit juices as they are the equivalent of eating 10 oranges in one go, giving you a huge sugar rush without the healthy fibre or pulp to go along with it.

Omega-3 fatty acids

We have been brainwashed into thinking that all fats are bad for us. However, despite containing more calories than carbs, the omega-3 fatty acids found in healthy fats, such as nuts, seeds, oily fish, spinach and avocados have been shown to break down fat.

Omega-3s cannot be manufactured by the body so it is essential that we include them in our diet as they perform many invaluable tasks, such as ensuring brain function and healthy eyesight and lowering the risks of heart disease and depression. These 'healthy fats' have also been shown to help people lose weight, particularly around the middle.

It's important to make sure you get a daily dose of healthy fats in your diet. While eating oily fish twice a week provides all the omega-3 fatty acids we need, you can also chop half an avocado into your salad, eat a handful of walnuts or sprinkle some linseeds on to your cereal. These are just some options that will ensure that you get your essential omega-3s, as well as providing you with plenty of healthy alternatives for a tasty, interesting and balanced diet.

Replacing the 'happy' drug

Serotonin, otherwise known as 'the happy hormone', is an important and essential hormone that elevates our mood. Low levels of serotonin have been linked to depression. Carbs play an essential role in producing and regulating serotonin, and studies have shown that people eating a high-carb diet produce more serotonin and are more relaxed as a result. This is why some people crave carbs and the self-medication it brings.

So what do you do if you are restricting or eliminating refined carbs from your diet? There are other foods that boost your serotonin levels, such as coriander, bananas, eggs, avocados and turkey. So make sure that you eat these foods regularly. Wholewheat carbs, such as brown rice or pasta, would also fit the bill.

Tips to speed up your metabolism

Your metabolism determines the rate at which you burn calories and fat. Therefore, the faster your metabolism, the quicker you will be able to lose weight. Here are some tips to speed up your metabolism:

- Eat regularly. Each time you restrict your food intake your metabolism drops as your body registers that food is in short supply, and therefore slows down your digestive system. Missing one meal a day can lower your metabolism by 15 per cent. This is another reason why starvation diets don't work – when you return to normal eating your metabolism has slowed right down, causing you to pile on the pounds even quicker than before.

- Get enough sleep. At least six hours of sleep a night encourages the right balance of the hormones linked to your metabolism.

- Take regular exercise (see Chapter 8 for tips). This is a sure-fire way to kickstart your metabolism.

- Your metabolic rate slows in a warmer environment so turn down the heating. At night, your body will work harder and therefore burn off more calories if you are in a cool room.

- Eat some protein at every meal as your body has to work harder to digest it, causing the rate of your metabolism to increase.

Revisiting your eating style

In Chapter 2 you took the eating style questionnaire and learned what type of eater you are. This chapter has already shown you which foods you should be cutting out of your diet as far as possible, as well as which foods you should be making part of your daily diet. Now I am going to provide you with very practical and specific solutions for the way you eat according to your eating style. The solutions below are split into exercises for your mind and top tips for the body.

Emotional Eater

If you are an Emotional Eater, it is likely that you are eating to fill a need that you are not having fulfilled elsewhere. It's important to understand that you are more than good enough and that comfort food will not make you feel better about yourself. The following exercise will help you to rebuild your self-esteem and to realise that you deserve as much love and respect as anyone else, from yourself as well as from others.

EXERCISE 12: *Who loves you, baby?*

Step 1: Close your eyes and think of someone who loves or deeply appreciates you. Take in everything about them – their clothes, their stance, what they are saying. Imagine they are standing in front of you right now.

Step 2: Now imagine floating out of your body and into theirs so that you are looking through their eyes. Feel the love and positive feelings they have for you as you look at yourself. Take in every detail of what they love or appreciate about you. Notice all those amazing qualities that perhaps you hadn't seen before.

Step 3: Float back into your own body, taking all that love and appreciation with you. Turn up the feelings throughout your body, holding on to the notion that you are never alone and that there are always people out there who you mean a lot to.

Step 4: Write down below what you learned from the exercise. You can repeat it whenever you need a boost – for example, when you are tempted to eat and you know you shouldn't. The more you do it, the more automatic the feelings become.

_____

_____

_____

_____

_____

_____

TOP BODY TIPS FOR EMOTIONAL EATERS:

- Plan ahead with your shopping and only buy what's on your list.
- Stop buying the snack foods and alcohol that are bad for you – if you don't have them in the house, you can't eat them!
- Make sure you have lots of healthy snacks in the house instead, e.g. fruit, nuts, raw vegetables, healthy dips.
- Give yourself non-edible treats for staying off the carbs and alcohol, such as a relaxing bath, reading a good book, listening to music or catching up with friends.

Big Eater

Big Eaters don't like waste. They always clear their own plates and often those of others as well. They also regularly opt for what they perceive to be value for money and tend to choose quantity over quality. If you're a Big Eater, the following exercise will help you to start eating more normal portion sizes.

EXERCISE 13: *In the tunnel*

It takes approximately a month for new conscious behaviours to become subconscious habits. If you are a Big Eater, every day for a month, ask yourself the question 'Am I feeling full yet?' whenever you eat a meal. (Make sure you eat slowly enough to allow yourself to realise you feel full, though!) Stop as soon as the answer is 'yes'. And, if you're not sure, just start to leave some food on your plate as that will teach your subconscious mind that it's OK to leave food there and still feel good about it!

At the end of the month, make a note below of how different you now feel about leaving food on your plate.

_____

_____

_____

_____

_____

_____

_____

TOP BODY TIPS FOR BIG EATERS:

- Use a smaller plate to help you reduce your portion size.

- Go for quality over quantity when it comes to your food. This will leave you feeling more satisfied and less likely to carry on eating.

- Recycle your food as much as possible so it's not being wasted.

- Tell yourself that you are in control and making your own choices about how best to eat.

- Remember that if you're eating out, you don't have to clear your plate just because you're paying for it. Try asking for smaller portions.

People Pleaser

If you are a People Pleaser, you like to keep everyone happy and find it tough to say no to foods that are not good for you. The following exercise will help you to become more assertive and put your own needs first.

EXERCISE 14: *Learning to say 'no'*

Step 1: Every day for a month, stand in front of a mirror and say, 'No thanks, it's not good for me. I'm going to eat something else.'

Step 2: Then start to say it for real whenever you're in a situation where you'd rather eat something else. This may be a night out with friends who are putting you under pressure to conform, a dinner party at a friend's house where you know they will have to accommodate you with something else or that special meal that your partner has cooked for you and you risk hurting their feelings. Remember that your needs are as important as theirs.

Step 3: Make a note below of how it felt to look after YOU for a change.

TOP BODY TIPS FOR PEOPLE PLEASERS:

- If you are going out for a meal, make sure you choose a restaurant that has a good variety of food.

- If you are going to a friend's house, tell them in advance what you like to eat.

- Explain to your partner why it's important to you to eat different foods in future.

- Remember that it's never too late to do something different.

Addictive Eater

If you are an Addictive Eater, you are compulsive around food. You overeat and undereat and always have food on your mind. You may also display obsessive behaviour. The following exercise aims to put an end to food ruling your life.

EXERCISE 15: *Regaining control*

Step 1: Make a list of the things you are missing out on in order to be able to eat indiscriminately. For example, you can't wear the clothes you want, you can't enjoy being on the beach, you are unfit and so on. Write everything down.

_____

_____

_____

_____

_____

_____

_____

_____

Now ask yourself whether the price is one worth paying. I'm certain that the answer will be no.

Step 2: Every day for a month, stand in front of a mirror and say, 'I love the feeling that I am in control now'. As you say this, notice how much you enjoy this feeling.

Step 3: Make a list of all the areas in your life where you choose to have certain restrictions placed on you, showing therefore that you can be in control. For example:

I am in a relationship and I happily accept the restrictions of no longer being single.

I am a parent and I happily accept the restrictions of everything that entails.

I have a mortgage and I happily accept the financial restrictions this places on me.

I work and happily accept the restrictions that makes on my social life.

And so on. Realise that there are many areas in your life in which you are successfully in control. Placing restrictions on what and how much you eat doesn't need to feel like a bad thing.

Step 4: Slowly reintroduce things in the house that you would normally binge on and notice how you can choose to be in control and restrict your consumption of them. Make a note below of how good it feels to be in control.

_____

_____

_____

_____

_____

_____

TOP BODY TIPS FOR ADDICTIVE EATERS:

- Plan each day's meals in advance to ensure you cook the right amount of healthy, nutritious food.

- Make sure you always have healthy snacks in the house.

- Keep busy to keep your mind off of food.

- Reward yourself by doing something you enjoy (non-edible rewards of course) when you demonstrate how much you are in control. (See previous examples under Emotional Eater.)

Lazy Eater

Food is a low priority for the Lazy Eater. You see food only as 'fuel' and don't make the time to eat properly. You put your health in second place to other priorities in your life. The following exercise will demonstrate to you the importance of looking after your body.

EXERCISE 16: *My body is my greatest gift*

Step 1: Write down what it will cost you if you don't change now.

_____

_____

_____

_____

_____

_____

Step 2: Get hold of two jars. Put a coin in the first jar each time you eat a healthy meal made up of the types of food recommended in this chapter. In the second jar add a coin each time you eat 'lazy' food. Notice at the end of the first week which jar has most coins in it. If it's the 'lazy' food jar, donate all the money to a charity. Keep going until you have two consecutive weeks where the first jar has the most coins. Make a note below of how that has changed your thoughts about food.

_____

_____

_____

_____

_____

_____

TOP BODY TIPS FOR LAZY EATERS:

- Plan, plan and plan again. Always work out in advance what you are going to eat each day and make sure you have the necessary ingredients at home.

- Order your food online from a supermarket that will deliver to your home, and save the list so that next time you can just change the odd item for variety.

- Only buy healthy foods.

- Drink alcohol only at the weekends and in moderation.

Control-Freak Eater

If you are a Control-Freak Eater, it is likely that you use food to feel more in control of your world or as a way of controlling others. You may also feel angry at times with your lot in the world. The following exercise aims to bring you inner calm and peace by helping you to express hurt and anger as close to them occurring as possible. By becoming used to expressing your hurt out loud, your body will not have to express it in a disguised or abnormal way, such as by overeating.

EXERCISE 17: *Learning to express yourself*

Step 1: Find a quiet room in the house where you have privacy. Say out loud what it is you are unhappy about. Say it over and over until the negative feelings disappear.

Step 2: When you are feeling angry or a situation feels out of your control, you must express those feelings. If someone else is able to do something about this, tell them how you feel. If not, it's up to you to find a way to take control of it as best you can.

Step 3: Every day for a month, say the following to yourself in front of a mirror: 'I express myself easily so my body doesn't have to do it for me.'

TOP BODY TIPS FOR CONTROL-FREAK EATERS:

- Only buy healthy food.
- Find time each day to relax, perhaps by listening to your favourite music or practising deep breathing.
- Each time you are able to freely express yourself, reward yourself with a non-edible treat such as a night out or a new item of clothing.

Pulling it all together

In this chapter we've explored both what not to eat and how to eat to be fit and healthy for the rest of your life. We've also explored specific tactics for each type of eater. So you've now got a lot to think about! In a moment you are going to have the chance to create your own new regime. But first go back over this chapter to refresh your memory about the specific changes you need to make to kick-start your new eating plan. This exercise is all about setting yourself specific goals in terms of the food and drink you will consume from now on.

EXERCISE 18: *My healthy lifestyle*

Step 1: List below what you are going to cut out of your diet (include food and drink):

_____

_____

_____

_____

_____

_____

_____

Step 2: List below what you are going to start eating:

_____

_____

_____

_____

_____

_____

_____

Step 3: List below what you are going to start drinking:

_____

_____

_____

_____

_____

_____

Step 4: List below how you will speed up your metabolism:

_____

_____

_____

_____

_____

Step 5: List below which of the eating style mind and body exercises you are going to start doing and how often:

_____

_____

_____

_____

_____

_____

_____

How did that feel? You have taken a key step towards your healthy future. And we all know how tough it can be to break old habits, so here are some tips to help you to keep on track:

- Make a decision to do the things you have just written down from this very moment. Remember you can change your destiny instantly once you make the decision to do something different. Tell yourself that you refuse to be one of those overweight people who are prepared to change everything except the way they eat! Make that commitment to yourself now.

- Focus on what you want and know that you can achieve it. Visualise your success like we did earlier in the book over and over until you absolutely know, feel and believe it will happen.

- Initiate change! Take a first step today. Transform your shopping trolley, change your drinking habits. You can do it.

- Persist. When things go off the rails, get back on track and restart. We all have off days, but being disciplined 80 per cent of the time will make a huge difference. Always keep what you're aiming for clear in your mind, which should help you to stay focused on your goals.

- Whenever you see yourself making real progress, such as dropping a clothes size, for example, reward yourself with something non-edible such as a new item of clothing or day out.

TIP: *Remember to always eat food as close to its natural state as possible.*

Banish Those Cravings for Good

The previous chapter was all about helping you to create your new healthy regime. This chapter is designed to help you stick to it! At the end of the day you are only human and there will be times when you are tempted to eat those foods that you know aren't good for your body. I'm going to give you some NLP strategies that will help you to keep you focused and in control when those weak moments come along.

I'm sure you've had lots of cravings before, so you'll be familiar with the feeling that when you get one it needs to be satisfied immediately. But a craving for a certain food is just a learned behaviour from the past. That means you weren't born with it and I can teach you techniques to unlearn these behaviours in an instant. Imagine if you could stop liking certain foods or drinks for ever? Sounds impossible? Well, I'm going to show you how. So what are you waiting for?

How to regulate your blood sugar

We all get cravings for sugar, especially when our blood-sugar levels are low or we aren't feeling too great.

You know that feeling when you start to get light-headed or irritable as your blood sugar drops and you typically reach out for a sugary snack to give you an instant boost? This can often happen mid- to late afternoon and late in the evening. The best way to prevent yourself from turning to sugary foods for a quick fix is to make sure your blood sugar remains stable in the first place. Here are a few tips on what you can do to avoid low blood-sugar levels:

- **Eat little and often.** This is an extremely important life change. Eating little and often is easy, and it enables you to stabilise your blood sugar by topping it up every three hours. Just make sure that you eat three meals a day – breakfast, lunch and dinner – as well as a mid-morning and mid-afternoon snack. Making sure your meals and snacks are healthy options (see Chapter 6 for a reminder) will allow your body to receive a slow and steady flow of energy, helping to keep your sugar level stable and keeping you fuller for longer. When you switch to this way of eating you'll notice these differences:

  — You will get your energy back.

  — Your cravings for sweet foods and refined carbs will stop. as your body will no longer need to get a quick fix. Once your blood sugar is steady you'll be amazed how easy it is to resist that piece of chocolate cake.

  — You'll also notice that you will experience far fewer mood swings and less irritability.

- **Eat breakfast.** The most important meal of the day; it's not called 'break-fast' for nothing. If you miss breakfast, your blood-sugar levels will drop within a few hours and you'll be looking for that quick fix. Allow yourself 10–15 minutes to sit down and eat a healthy breakfast. Meals like porridge (not the instant type), no-added sugar muesli or scrambled eggs will give you a steady level of blood sugar throughout the morning.

> **TIP:** *Add cinnamon to your porridge as it is known to improve the transport of glucose to the cells, thereby keeping up your energy levels.*

- **Eliminate all sugar and refined carbs from your diet for at least 80 per cent of the time.** See the previous chapter for more information on this.
- **Add protein to each meal.** As soon as you add a protein (animal or vegetable) to a carbohydrate, you make your body work harder to break down your food, meaning that the energy will be released more slowly and you'll stay fuller for longer.

> **TIP:** *Adding protein to a meal can be as simple as tossing a handful of nuts onto your porridge, eating a hard-boiled egg alongside your soup or topping your jacket potato with tuna.*

- **Don't eat on the run.** If you persistently eat on the run, you give your body the message that time is short, that you are under pressure and that you are stressed. Tell it instead that all is well and that you are fine by taking more time over your meals. Chewing your food well is also important as it gives you more opportunity to notice that you are full and you will therefore be less likely to overeat.

- **Reduce caffeine.** As mentioned before, coffee, black tea, green tea, chocolate, colas and energy drinks all contain caffeine. Caffeine affects cravings for food because it raises the stress hormone cortisol. Cortisol raises your heart rate and blood pressure and tells your body to increase energy stores. This results in the body craving sweet things. So if you're wondering why you're craving a biscuit in the after-noon, it could be something to do with that coffee you drank with breakfast. Replace with water or fruit teas. If you really can't go without tea or coffee, drink decaffeinated varieties instead.

Alternative treats

If you have sugar cravings it's important to remember that highly refined sugar, such as that found in biscuits, cakes, etc., is not food at all, it is a chemical. Sugar makes you fat, ages your skin, rots your teeth, disrupts your digestion and is extremely addictive. It doesn't really have much going for it, does it?

If you get a sugar craving that you really can't overcome, there are other more naturally sweet foods that will help that do not have the same negative effects on your body as refined sugar. You just need to make sure that you have a supply in the house and in your handbag or briefcase. Naturally sweet snacks include all fresh fruit, dried fruit such as figs, dates, and apricots, soya yoghurt bars and soya shakes.

> **TIP:** *Many people who crave sugar are low in zinc or magnesium. Eating zinc-rich foods such as prawns, eggs and pumpkin seeds, or magnesium-rich foods such as apples, avocados, Brazil nuts, almonds and broccoli, can make it easier for you to overcome cravings. Alternatively, you could take a supplement of each.*

Pleasure or pain? How to beat your cravings

Have you ever had a time in the past when you have eaten something and enjoyed it at the time, then afterwards you've had food poisoning and you ended up with your head down the loo? Once you've recovered, the last thing you want to eat is whatever has just caused your food poisoning! In NLP terms, your brain has permanently linked the pain of the event, i.e. the food poisoning, to the food, so that when you think of that food in future you feel like throwing up. In fact, some people can never look at, smell, touch or be around a food that made them ill ever again. I remember a time as a very small child travelling to stay with my aunt in Holland. My family arrived late and we were all very tired from the journey. My aunt had made a casserole and I was violently ill after eating it. Even now, 40 years later, my stomach still churns if I smell a certain type of casserole and I immediately get an image in my head of the event, despite the fact it was so very long ago.

Think of a food now that you simply cannot eat. If you don't have one, think of something you've never eaten but couldn't possibly imagine eating, such as tripe, kidney, black pudding or brain! Now think about why you cannot eat it. You'll notice that it's the smell, taste or texture of the food in your mouth, or maybe even all three. This feeling of revulsion occurs naturally and subconsciously. Since this is something you can already do, I am now going to teach you how to apply this technique consciously to other foods that you want to stop eating or drinking. In NLP terms we call this 'away from' motivation because we are motivated by avoiding what we don't want. The opposite is 'towards' motivation which is what we used in Exercise 4 when you created your vision board and goals for the future. That time you linked pleasure to your goals, whereas now you are using pain to achieve your objective.

The following exercises will help you to effect change

both at a conscious and subconscious level. Only do them if you want to stop eating a particular food or particular drink for good. Pick a food or drink that you enjoy bingeing on; one of those foods you would reach for in a sugar-craving moment. Popular choices are chocolate, bread, biscuits, sweets, white wine or red wine. Be specific.

EXERCISE 19: *Anchoring for success*

Read through all the steps before we start. If you would prefer to listen to a recording of this and the following two exercises, visit my website at www.thechangecorporation.com or www.lindseyagness.com, where you can download one of me taking you through the process.

Step 1: Think of a food or drink you hate – one that really revolts you. You can make it so that it's gone off for even more effect! You should be on the point of retching as you think about it now.

Step 2: Now vividly imagine a plate of that food or a glass of that drink right in front of you. Imagine smelling it and then putting some large mouthfuls right into your mouth and on to your tongue. Notice the texture of it in your mouth. As you start to feel awful, squeeze your thumb and index finger together. Keep your fingers squeezed together until you start to feel better (typically up to 15 seconds). Repeat several times, ramping up your revulsion each time. When you are nauseous, stop and relax your fingers.

Step 3: Now think of the food or drink you crave and notice that you have a picture of you eating or drinking it in your mind.

Step 4: Now make that picture of you eating or drinking it much bigger and brighter. Imagine turning up the dials on the colour, brightness and size, and bring it closer and closer to you.

Step 5: Now this is the exciting part! While you have the picture of the food or drink you like in your mind, squeeze your thumb and index finger together. Remember the taste and texture of the food or drink you hate and imagine some of it mixed in with the food or drink you love. Notice how the food or drink you like begins to change now. Imagine eating both foods together; think about the taste and texture. Keep eating them both in your mind and imagine swallowing them down and how awful they taste. Keep squeezing your thumb and index finger together as you eat. Continue until you can't eat any more it's so awful. Then stop.

Step 6: Think about that food you used to like and notice how you feel differently about it now. You can repeat this process as often as you like until you have completely eliminated your desire for that particular food.

EXERCISE 20: *Like to dislike*

This is another process for swapping a food you like into a food you dislike. Read all the steps before you make a start. The objective is for the food you currently like to become a food that you are repulsed by, so only do this on foods that you are happy to give up permanently.

Step 1: As you think about the food or drink you love and wished you didn't, notice that you have a picture of it in your mind. When I say 'picture', I don't mean an image of it as clear as a photograph. What I mean is rather for you to get a 'sensation' of it and to notice that it has a location in relation to your body. So if I were to ask you where that food or drink is, in what direction would you point? You may notice it in front of you, to one side, behind you. Any location is perfect. You should also pay attention to:

- Whether it's in black and white or colour
- How big it is
- Whether you can see yourself in the picture or if you're looking through your own eyes

Are there any sounds associated with this picture? If there are, notice if:

- They are loud or soft

- They are fast or slow

- There is anything special or unique about them

Then clear the picture from your mind.

Step 2: Now think of a food or drink that you find absolutely revolting. (If you are already working on a food, pick another food and if you are already working on a drink, pick another drink etc.) A food or drink that you feel sick just thinking about. You can make it mouldy or rancid for even greater effect! Notice that you have a picture in your mind. Go through the same process as before. Then clear the picture from your mind.

Step 3: Here comes the interesting part! Compare both lists of features. If it makes it easier, write them down. Then mark each feature that is different. For example, the first picture may be in colour while the second is in black and white, or the first picture may be out in front of you while the second is to your side and just above the floor. Highlight **all** the differences.

Step 4: Now get back that old picture of the food you want to dislike and change it into all the elements of the second picture that are different. For example, if the first picture is in colour and the second is in black and white, take the colour out of the first picture so that it is also black and white. If the location is different, move the first picture to the location of the second. In the example above, you would move the picture from in front of you to your side and just above the floor. Notice how easily you can do this – the brain learns fast. Keep going until the first picture has all the same features as the second picture. You will notice that, at some point, you will feel very differently about the first food or drink. It will begin to lose its attraction to you and eventually become repulsive. That's how you know the exercise has been a success. Keep going until you are finished. You can repeat this exercise on any food or drink you wish to give up. Just remember that it is a permanent process.

I am now going to show you how to reprogramme your brain to change what you eat or drink if you get a craving. So if you normally crave a biscuit or a beer, you can teach your brain to tell you to reach for an apple or a fizzy water instead. And you won't even feel like you're depriving yourself. Very clever!

EXERCISE 21: *Swishing to success*

It's easier if you have a partner for this exercise, especially the first time you do it. Tell your partner upfront what it is you want to stop craving. It's important that you and your partner read through all the steps before you begin so the whole thing runs as smoothly as possible.

Step 1: Your partner asks you, 'How do you know it's time to crave _____ (e.g. a biscuit)?' You should identify your trigger point for this particular craving, such as late at night when you're lonely, or mid-afternoon when you're working at your desk. It's important for you to be as specific as possible about this.

Your partner should then ask you, 'When you think of _____ (your trigger point), do you have a picture of that situation in your mind?' Your partner then tells you to clear your mind of that picture by asking you a random question such as, 'What did you have for breakfast today?'

Step 2: Your partner then asks you, 'What would you like to eat/drink instead?' Think of a healthier alternative, e.g. an apple, and tell your partner, who will then ask you, 'When you think of that _____ (food or drink item), do you have a picture in your mind of you eating it?'

Step 3: Your partner then tells you to turn up the brightness of the second picture, to make it bigger, and to bring it closer to you until it is very appealing to you. You should be looking through your own eyes in this picture. Once it is at its most appealing, your partner asks you to step out of the picture so you now see yourself in it. They then ask you to clear your mind as before.

Step 4: Now your partner guides you to bring back the first picture, making sure that you are looking through your own eyes again. This picture should be right out in front of you.

Step 5: You put the second picture, small and dark, down by your left-hand side at floor level. Make sure you see yourself in the picture.

Step 6: Your partner then tells you to increase the size of the new picture until it covers the old picture, which shrinks down and becomes small and dark in your lower left-hand corner. You should do this as your partner says the word 'sssswishhhhh' at speed.

Step 7: Your partner asks you to open your eyes and clear your mind of either picture.

Step 8: You should now get your partner to help you repeat steps 3–6 until you can no longer access the picture of you eating the food or drink you are giving up. You can only see the picture of you with the healthy alternative.

Step 9: Your partner tests that it has worked by asking you about your trigger point, e.g. 'Imagine it's late and you're lonely. How is your craving different now? What do you want to eat instead?' If necessary, repeat the exercise until the picture of the unhealthy item has completely disappeared.

Terry – taking control of his cravings

Terry is a member of the control group. He is 43 and weighed 17st 4lbs at the start of our work together. Terry's biggest weight-loss challenge was his two-hour journey back home from work each day. He had got into the bad habit of using a petrol stop to feed his craving for carbohydrates. He was hungry, bored and tired and so it was easy to let temptation get the better of him. His biggest downfalls were chocolate, diet cola and biscuits. He could quite easily buy a chocolate bar, several cans of cola and a packet of biscuits and eat them all before he got home.

Terry knew that he couldn't continue eating in this way. He did the Like to Dislike exercise on chocolate first of all, which worked so well that he could no longer even think about it. The trouble was that he began to eat more biscuits, so he then did the exercise on biscuits too, which helped him to give them up completely. Diet cola was next to go and he hasn't drunk it since.

He then used the Swish exercise to swap his craving for lager into soda water, which has proved 100 per cent effective for him. He found that these NLP exercises have played a major role in helping him to get his cravings under control and he is consequently well on the way to achieving a healthier weight.

Change your language, change your future

As we know, the 'L' in NLP stands for linguistic and relates to the effect our language has on our feelings and our actions. Our subconscious mind takes what we say literally, so if you say to yourself, 'I'm famished', your brain will encourage you to overeat. Often the words we use mask the real problem, meaning that when we tell ourselves that we feel hunger, very often this isn't the case at all. What we are really feeling is sadness, loneliness, boredom or stress.

So next time you have a craving, ask yourself, 'Am I really hungry or am I feeling a different emotion?' Be honest with yourself. If it's not hunger then tell yourself instead, 'I am in control of what I eat and I do not need to eat now.' Then deal with the emotion. Whatever you tell yourself, your mind will absorb and accept. If you change your language, you will change how you feel in an instant. Getting into the habit of telling yourself positive messages is very effective at helping you to avoid unnecessary eating and in dealing with the real emotions you are feeling. If you are lonely, arrange to see a friend or pick up the phone to someone you haven't spoken to in a while. If you are miserable, do something that will cheer you up, such as treating yourself to something. If you are stressed, go for a walk or practise deep breathing. And if you're bored, plan a night out to give you something to look forward to. The important thing is to break the pattern by doing something different.

Janice – socialising to lose weight

Janice, aged 50, has time on her hands. Both of her children have recently left home and she now lives alone. She is an Emotional Eater who often finds herself craving sweet and sugary foods late at night. I asked her to note the feelings she felt immediately before she ate any of the foods she craved. Although she realised that she thought about food a lot of the time, she discovered that she was not really hungry at the moment her cravings hit. She learned instead that she eats when she is bored and lonely. We discussed some new strategies for her and she is now reconnecting with old friends. She has started to go out again a couple of nights a week and has taken up salsa dancing at the weekends. The result is that her occupied mind now thinks less about food and her urge to snack on the wrong foods has naturally evaporated as she has become busier and busier.

Pulling it all together

In this chapter we've explored tactics to help you take complete control of your cravings. Remember that all cravings are just learned behaviours and you can unlearn them easily. The exercises I've shared with you in this chapter will eliminate cravings in no time at all. If you don't yet believe me, do them all a couple more times and begin to feel in complete control of what you eat. You may need a partner to work with the first time, but once you become familiar with these techniques you can use them on yourself. We've also explored how to make sure your blood-sugar levels are regulated so you are less likely to experience a craving in the first place. And, if you've discovered that your craving isn't really hunger at all but an altogether different feeling like loneliness, boredom, stress and so on, then deal with what's really going on. If you need some help with this, go back to Chapter 4 and do Exercises 7 and 8 on changing your personal history and letting go of negative emotions. Then simply sit back and enjoy the results!

> **TIP:** *Stop buying the foods you crave so you are never even tempted! Buy healthy alternatives instead.*

Exercise: The Dreaded E-word

We've all heard the expression 'No pain, no gain', but exercise doesn't have to be painful, or boring for that matter. Anything that increases your heart rate and encourages you to breathe more deeply can be classed as exercise, and I bet you can think of a few such things now that you love to do. Maybe you like to go for long walks or to a salsa class? If you like to go to the gym five times a week, great. But you don't have to do that. You already exercise to a certain extent every day simply by moving about. The key is to move around more than you do now.

So you will need to put in some effort – think of it not as 'no pain, no gain' but rather 'no effort, no gain' – but there are plenty of fun and enjoyable ways you can introduce exercise into your life.

The physical benefits of regular exercise

There is no doubt that exercise is a crucial part of any weight-loss regime, and there is also overwhelming evidence that people who lead active lifestyles are less likely to suffer from illness and more likely to live longer. Here are just some of the many physical benefits of exercise. It:

- Tones and firms muscles, improving body shape
- Increases energy, strength and stamina
- Reduces risk of osteoporosis and certain cancers
- Strengthens the heart, thereby reducing the risk of heart disease
- Improves circulation
- Strengthens the immune system
- Improves liver function
- Increases level of enzymes in body that burn fat
- Lowers blood pressure
- Lowers resting heart rate
- Increases metabolic rate, thereby helping you to burn more calories even when you're at rest
- Reduces joint discomfort and improves flexibility

The psychological benefits of exercise

Exercise not only makes you physically fitter; it also improves your mental health and general sense of well-being. The psychological benefits of regular exercise can be as significant as the physical, if not more so. Some, such as increased self-esteem, come as an indirect result of exercise, i.e. we become happier in ourselves once we lose weight and our body shape changes. Others are a direct consequence of chemical activity triggered by physical exertion. Brain chemicals released during exercise, such as serotonin, dopamine and endorphins, are known to have strong effects on mood, helping reduce feelings of anxiety, stress and depression.

Twenty different types of endorphin have been discovered in the nervous system, and the beta-endorphins secreted during exercise have the most powerful effect. Sometimes described as a 'runner's high', the release of beta-endorphins reduces pain (the reason why running becomes easier after about 20 minutes) and stimulates feelings of euphoria, which is why so many people feel invigorated and enthusiastic after exercise. In fact, any time you want a boost, just take 10 to 15 minutes' exercise that gets your heart rate going and breathing more deeply than you do when sedentary and it will work wonders. When it can feel like exercise is the last thing in the world that will cheer you up, remember that it is one of the very best ways to do just that.

The main psychological benefits of exercise are that it:

- Improves self-esteem and self-confidence

- Improves mental focus

- Reduces risk of depression

- Decreases overall feelings of stress and tension

- Improves quality of sleep

How to get started

The government recommends a minimum of 30 minutes of moderate-intensity exercise 5 times a week. This means raising your heart rate to a level where you are moderately breathless. As I said earlier, you don't need to spend hours at the gym or run marathons to be fit and healthy. Also, bear in mind that you can do three 10-minute or two 15-minute bouts to reach your minimum of 30 minutes. Short bursts of activity can be as effective as lengthier sessions and you might find this a more manageable target to begin with.

The easiest way to sustain an exercise regime is to find activities that can be incorporated into your daily routine so that they become a habit. Ways to raise your level of physical activity include:

- Increasing the number of steps you take per day (buy a simple pedometer at any sports shop)
- Cycling or walking to work a few days each week
- Walking up moving escalators
- Using the stairs instead of the lift
- Taking brisk walks during your lunch hour
- Getting off the bus one or two stops earlier than usual and walking the rest of the way
- Taking up a sport you enjoy, e.g. jogging, swimming, cycling, canoeing

- Taking up a new activity, e.g. dancing, yoga, Pilates, pole dancing!
- Going to the gym
- Doing the housework or gardening
- Dancing to your favourite music
- And, of course, having more sex!

Sometimes it's hard to motivate yourself to be more physically active and it can feel like a chore. So the easiest way to start is by changing the way you think about regular exercise. Tell yourself that it is fun and that you enjoy it. Remember that if you tell yourself, 'I hate this' or 'It hurts' or 'I don't like this', you are giving your subconscious mind a message to give up. If you say instead, 'I am choosing this because I am choosing to be thinner' or 'I can do it, I will do it', these positive statements will keep you going. Even if this isn't an absolute fact at the start, it will become one very quickly. Keep reminding yourself that it will make you feel better, and will improve the quality and length of your life.

It's also important that you start at your own pace. If you have never exercised before, you will start on a different level than someone who stopped exercising five years ago. The key is to get started and not to compare yourself to anyone else. You'll soon discover that a brisk walk in nature is refreshing, a salsa class is vibrant and exhilarating, a swim is calming. Most importantly, all of these activities can be fun!

You may also find it easier if you have support with your exercise programme. Very few people can do it entirely alone. Go to the gym with a friend, find a running buddy or go dancing with your partner. Motivating each other to do more exercise will benefit you both. If you can, you may want to hire a personal trainer. They are very good at keeping you on track and will not let you off the hook when your motivation begins to wane.

My fitness track record

When I was overweight at school I hated sports day. In fact, I remember hiding in the girls' toilets to avoid having to enter any of the races. I carried this loathing into adulthood until the day I met my now ex-husband. I was on a management course out in the country. I remember one morning looking out of my window and seeing one of the other students, a handsome, tall and athletic figure running into the courtyard in front of my room. He was sweating profusely and I wondered why on earth anyone would choose to run for fun! Once we started dating I discovered that he was into every sport going. It seemed that the only way I would ever see him was to join in one of the activities. I tried windsailing and kept having to be rescued from the middle of the lake, totally incapable of reading the wind to get myself back to dry land. I tried karate but that was too rough for me. I tried squash but found it too competitive and so it came down to running.

I arrived at the running club that he was a member of for my first run. I was slim, yet hadn't ever really run in my life. I'll always remember the poor chap who got the short straw that night when he was asked to run with me around the block – literally a few hundred yards. By the time I got back my face was as red as a beetroot and I thought I was going to have a heart attack! My ex thought it was hilarious, of course! However, I persevered as I wanted to see him and soon I was running a mile, then two and so on. The next year I ran my first marathon and eventually I became a more enthusiastic runner than he was. Although I no longer run marathons, I make sure running is in my schedule two or three times a week. I run for between 30 minutes and an hour and I love it. I enjoy being in the fresh air and I love the flexibility of running – I take my running shoes wherever I travel as it's a great way of exploring a new city or town. Running is now in my blood, it's part of my routine and it's a discipline that I hope I'll always be fit enough to enjoy. I guess the moral is that we all have to start somewhere. I could so easily have given up that first night but I didn't. I had the motivation of my new relationship. You have the motivation of your new body!

EXERCISE 22: *Your exercise goals*

You need to set yourself short- and long-term exercise goals. The importance of short-term goals is that success in these will provide you with a sense of satisfaction and further motivation to keep up the new lifestyle, ultimately helping you to achieve your long-term goals. Keep your goals specific, measurable, achievable, realistic and time-based (SMART). For example, rather than saying you will get fit by summer, start by setting the more specific goal of going to a one-hour aerobics or yoga class each week. Write down your answers to the following questions:

What new activities are you going to begin?

_____

_____

_____

What activities do you already do that you can do more of?

_____

_____

_____

How often will you do these things?

_____

_____

_____

For how long?

_____

_____

_____

What's your ultimate exercise aim, however far away it may be at the moment?

_____

_____

_____

What's your level of commitment (from 1–10, 1 = low, 10 = high) towards becoming fitter? If it's anything less than 10, re-read this chapter. Instilling new habits in yourself takes effort and commitment, so you need to be up for the challenge!

_____

_____

_____

Now the most important thing is to get started. So what are you waiting for? Put this book down for as long as it takes for you to take that first step. You'll feel so much better for it once it's done. I guarantee that it gets easier once your levels of fitness start to build – and the good news is that with regular effort you'll notice your fitness levels improving very quickly. Just imagine, no longer will you feel breathless as you climb those stairs and you'll be able to run for the bus or chase the kids round the garden. The first few times at anything new will take more effort, but keep in mind that end goal.

How to stay motivated

If you're anything like me, it's likely there will be certain days when it's harder to find the motivation to get active than others. For me it's the dark or rainy mornings! Here are some practical tips to help keep up your enthusiasm.

- Keep an exercise diary. The following are examples of what you might include:

  —How far you walked, ran, swam, cycled, etc.

  —How long you spent doing it

  —How you felt at the end

  —How you felt the next day

  This is great for improving your motivation as you can look back and see how you have improved over time. When I was training for my marathons I logged every run, how far I ran and how I felt at the end of each. I was inspired each time I discovered that I had run one of my routine runs faster and easier. You will feel the same when you notice yourself getting fitter.

- A great way to stay focused is to keep reminding yourself of the reasons you started exercising in the first place. Look at your Vision Board every day as that will keep your mind on your end goal. You can also collect inspirational stories from people who have achieved their weight goals – if they can do it, so can you.

- Visualise yourself achieving your goal weight. Imagine what it will feel like when, for example, you can finally fit into your smaller jeans again. Will you feel more confident? More ready for a new and exciting challenge? Imagine floating right into the thinner you and really absorb how it feels to be that person. Notice what you see and hear and how the world looks now looks to you from this thinner perspective. Visualising these images and feelings will motivate you by reprogramming your subconscious mind to support you in achieving your goal.

- As we now know, exercise releases chemicals called endorphins in the brain. These have a strong effect on your mood, helping to reduce anxiety, stress and depression. So whenever you don't feel like exercising, remind yourself of how good you'll feel afterwards. I use this one a lot!

Of course, if you have a medical condition and are concerned that you may hurt yourself exercising, talk to your GP. They will provide simple guidance on the benefits and types of activity that you can do safely and easily.

If you are still lacking motivation, the next two exercises will get you up and moving about in no time at all!

EXERCISE 23: *Moving from procrastination to motivation in an instant*

Step 1: Think about that activity that you are procrastinating about. As you think about it, notice that you have a picture of it. By picture, I don't mean a picture as clear as a photograph. What I mean is an image of yourself doing that activity, and it should have a particular location in some direction in relation to your body. So, if I were to ask you, 'Where is the picture?' to which direction would you point? You may notice it in front of you, to one side, or behind you. Any location is fine. Now clear your mind and remove the picture.

Step 2: Now think of something you are totally motivated about. That might be going on holiday, winning the lottery, etc. As you think about it, notice that you have a different picture. What is the location of that picture? Notice that it's different to the first picture. (If the location is not significantly different, think of other things you are motivated about until you find one where the location is different.) Clear your mind and remove the picture.

Step 3: Now bring back the picture of the situation you are procrastinating about and move it into the same position as the thing you are totally motivated about. Notice what happens. You immediately feel more motivated to do the task you used to procrastinate about.

That was easy wasn't it! I always use this technique to motivate myself when I'm procrastinating about something. It works for everything, not just exercise, so you may find yourself using it a lot from now on!

EXERCISE 24: *Anchoring that motivation*

Step 1: Remember specific occasions in the past when you were motivated or were doing something you love. Examples could be spending time with your family, going on a date or taking your partner for a romantic meal. Remember specific times, not just general feelings. Come up with at least six times and list them below.

Step 2: Take one specific memory from the list and return to it in your mind. Imagine floating down into your body and looking through your own eyes. See what you saw, hear what you heard and *really* feel those feelings of being totally

motivated and feeling happy. Make the colours brighter, the sounds louder and the feelings even stronger. As you get to the height of the memory and the pictures, sounds and feelings are as strong as they can be, apply pressure to the knuckle of your second finger on your left hand with the first finger of your right hand. (N.B. This is important – you need to use a different knuckle to the one we used in Exercise 7.) Continue to apply pressure to the knuckle as you relive the memory through your own eyes. As the pictures, sounds, feelings begin to ebb away, remove your finger from your knuckle. Clear the screen and think of something completely different for a moment, like what you are having for dinner! Repeat this for each of your powerful positive situations.

Step 3: Test – Now fire off the anchor by pressing the knuckle in exactly the same way without accessing a specific memory this time and notice how differently you feel. You will feel a combination of all the powerful positive states you just anchored to that knuckle. I'm sure, you will feel motivated and raring to go!

Step 4: Now when you want to exercise, fire off your motivation anchor. Notice how you immediately feel more motivated to go and do something. Keep practising this technique, adding more positive memories until you feel differently.

Jean – light on her feet, and the scales!

Jean is one of my control-group clients. She is 50 and weighed just under 16 stone at the start of the project. Her goal is to reach her ideal weight of 10.5 stone. She has always eaten relatively healthily, cooking most of her meals from scratch, but had a tendency to indulge in the occasional sugary treat. Despite having quite a healthy diet, however, she has continued to put on weight as she has got older.

Jean knew that her metabolism had slowed down considerably and that the only way she would shed her extra weight would be to exercise, although she lacked the motivation to do so. She is a teacher and arrives home earlier than her husband, who is also away three nights a week. Her daughter has recently left home so Jean has lots of time on her hands to be able to start and maintain and exercise regime. Jean's problem was, however, that whenever she decided to start exercising, she thought she had to go to the gym, go running or go swimming, all of which she hates. She had been a member of the local gym for the past three years but had only been there a handful of times!

Jean used the motivation exercises to increase her willpower, and we worked together to help her find activities she actually enjoyed. Although she'd only ever danced at parties or weddings, Jean realised that she loves to move to music as she enjoys the sense of freedom it gives her. As a result, she has joined a salsa class, which she goes to twice a week with a friend, and three times a week she follows an exercise DVD in her living room that uses disco dancing to help you lose weight and tone up. She has been following her new exercise regime for the past two months, and has no intention of stopping it any time soon. So far she has lost 1.5 stone, has dropped two dress sizes and feels healthier and happier than she has in a long time.

Pulling it all together

Remember that you only have one body and that exercise is good for you. Even if you've never exercised before, all you need to do is to begin. The rest will follow. It's never too late to start; you just have to take that first step. Get started now and have fun! A combination of a positive mindset, healthy eating and exercise is the real secret to weight loss.

> **TIP:** *The quicker you get into an exercise routine, the faster it will become a habit.*

CONCLUSION

How to Get Thin and Stay Thin

So we are almost at the end of our journey together. I have now given you all the tools you need to tackle your weight issues and I hope that you're feeling motivated to make the necessary changes so you can be who you want to be once and for all.

If you've not yet finished all the exercises, go back and fill in any of the gaps as it's these that really embed everything you've learned at both a conscious and a subconscious level.

There are four different stages involved when we integrate change permanently into our nervous system. It's not possible to jump stages, and if you fail to practise your new behaviours, you run the risk of falling back to a lower-level stage. Moving from stage to stage is often accompanied by a feeling of awakening or a feeling that 'the penny has dropped', and it can be very motivating to know that you have made such a big leap forwards.

Read through the four stages below and ask yourself where you are right now. You will be at least at stage two by the mere fact that you have read this book and completed the exercises! Wherever you find yourself at this point in time is perfect for the journey ahead, and it's now up to you to ensure that you keep moving forwards. You will only move up through further stages by taking action every day, such as making small changes to your behaviour or running through the exercises again, until these new practices feel 'normal' for you. If you find yourself falling back to earlier habits, notice what is happening, pick yourself up and keep going. This is not a time for recriminations; focus instead on what you can learn from the glitch to enable you to move forwards in a permanent way next time. You have everything you need in this book to help you keep going and get you to your destination – all you need now is the belief that you will get there!

- **Stage one: unconscious incompetence**
  This is where you were before you read this book. You may not have known that you were living life unhealthily or that you were doing damage to your body, and you didn't know how to change your bad habits.

- **Stage two: conscious incompetence**
  As you read the book you became aware of the possibilities for changing your lifestyle and becoming fit for life. However, you are still practising the new techniques and learning as you go. You still forget sometimes and go back to your old ways.

- **Stage three: conscious competence**
  This is where you are actively using the techniques for

eating, drinking and exercise. However, the new techniques have not yet become embedded as habits.

- **Stage four: unconscious competence**
  We now know that all long-term behavioural change has to take place at a subconscious level. When this happens, you have reached the fourth and final stage. This stage is where you have practised the new techniques so often that you do them all without having to think about it. Your new regime is now who you are and you no longer fall back into old ways except when you choose to on special occasions.

How to make sure you reach that final goal

Over the years, I've worked with a large number of very different people from different backgrounds, yet the same things have proven time and time again to help them maintain the motivation necessary to make changes to their lifestyles and attitudes so that they can achieve their ultimate weight-loss goals. They are all easy, practical steps that I've already discussed in this book and summarised here so you can refer back to this section whenever you need to.

I've always found one of the most powerful tools in helping people lose weight is the Vision Board. Keep yours somewhere where you can easily see it every day, and take the time really to absorb the feelings you get when you imagine achieving the goal your board portrays. As you come across more inspiring pictures, quotes, etc., continue to add them to your board – it should evolve with you as you move through the different stages of change.

The food diary has also always proved to be extremely useful as it is a quick and easy way to see where you are going wrong and to discover those all-important feelings that trigger bad eating habits. You should continue to keep your food diary on and off throughout this process of change, and looking back at it regularly should give you the inspiration to keep up the good work!

I've also found that it helps considerably to have a 'buddy' who is going through the same process as you as they act as a nudge to keep you on track. There are two ways in which this seems to help: firstly, verbalising your goals out loud to someone else helps to cement them in your mind, and, secondly, that external sense of commitment to your buddy gives you additional motivation not to fail in achieving your goals. I've always found that those with the best results used their buddy relationship consistently throughout the weight-loss process.

Another key predictor of long-term success is to aim for slow and steady progress rather than rushing into too many changes at once. For sustainable, successful weight loss, aim for 1–2 pounds a week, though the loss is likely to be greater in the first few weeks. And, the more overweight you are, the easier it is to shed those initial pounds.

In terms of diet, cutting back on carbs and alcohol has been proven to make the biggest and fastest difference to those aiming to lose weight and the small changes quickly add up. For example, one less 50 calorie plain biscuit a day could help you to lose 5 pounds (2.3 kg) in a year, so if you eat three biscuits a day at the moment, just cutting those out would help you to lose a stone! Another simple trick is to add protein to every meal. As soon as you add protein to a carb you change it into a slow-releasing carb, which prevents it from causing huge fluctuations in blood sugar, making it less likely that you will crave a quick sugar fix and thereby helping you to stay more in control of your food intake. You should also cut back on portion size and eat from a smaller plate. Eating a bit less makes a big difference in the long run and you'll be surprised by how quickly your body adjusts to the smaller portions. Cutting carbs out after lunch and especially in the evenings is another way to get the results you want fast. For example, having an evening meal of meat or fish with a salad or fresh vegetables will help with your late-night digestion process. Drinking water late at night or drinking a glass of ice-cold milk (not cow's milk!) was also found to take the edge off hunger pangs and cravings.

Planning ahead has also been shown to be key in helping my clients keep to their new food regime. This is especially important for Lazy Eaters. Once you have worked out a new set of menus, it is easy to plan ahead by putting aside an evening a week to do the shopping, making sure you stick rigidly to what's on your new shopping list, or by using a local supermarket delivery service. Also, ensure that you buy your core foodstuffs and snacks in bulk so that you don't run out of them and make sure that you stop buying the 'wrong' foods, even for others in your household, as it just leads to temptation for you. It's important always to carry healthy 'portable' snacks with you each day for your car, office, gym bag, etc. This will help you to avoid any temptation to stop and buy the wrong snack at the local petrol station or to be tempted when the Friday afternoon cakes come round at the office.

Another consistently important element of my clients' success has been when they have learned to put themselves first. For example, they found that calling in advance and warning friends that there are certain things they no longer wish to eat has taken any potential awkwardness out of a dinner party or a meal out. At restaurants, they have got used to asking for an alternative dish and 99 per cent of the time they have found it's not been an issue. If you think about it, it's no different if you are a vegetarian – you get used to asking for appropriate foods because you and your beliefs are worth it.

In terms of exercise, finding activities that you actually enjoy doing, whether that's walking in the countryside, swimming, joining a Pilates class or learning to salsa, is essential if you are to maintain your new exercise regime.

Tactics such as watching movies on your iPhone or using an exercise 'app' while at the gym may also help to keep you motivated.

And last but not least, getting yourself out of the house, starting new activities and reconnecting with friends may be just what you need to keep your mind off eating and help you achieve the weight loss you're aiming for.

EXERCISE 25: *My own top tips for health*

In this final exercise I want you to think about ten ways in which you feel you will be able to maintain your motivation throughout your weight-loss process. You can pull out ideas from the examples above, add your own or think back to the concepts covered in this book that have had the most impact on you, such as, 'Focus on what you want, not what you don't want' or, 'Constantly visualise yourself being thinner'. These ten ideas will then form the basis of your own successful 'Get Thin' campaign! Make a note of them below:

1. _____

2. _____

3. _____

4. _____

5. _____

6. _____

7. _____

8. _____

9. _____

10. _____

My final words

Keep in mind that this is not an ending, it's a new beginning. You have come so far already and will continue to make progress every day. I've enjoyed being with you on this journey and I really hope that I've inspired you to live a long, fit and healthy life.

Change starts from within and making a commitment to yourself that you are going to begin your new way of life now. Maybe these are changes that you'll make not only for yourself but for your whole family. Whatever you decide, and whatever your ultimate goals, every journey starts with a small step so take that first step today. Go out and buy healthier foods, cut down on your alcohol intake and get your body moving again. It gets easier and easier as you make progress every day.

I've shown you how to set goals for yourself, visualise your success and stop those cravings; I've also opened your eyes as to what you should and shouldn't eat and drink, and how you can make exercise an enjoyable and integral part of your life. So now, it's down to you. It's important that you read this book from cover to cover and do all the exercises, so if you've skipped any of them go back and do them now. They form part of your commitment to yourself to get healthy. Your body is the vessel through which you enjoy a long and happy life – if you compromise your health, you compromise your ability to become successful, achieve your personal goals and help others. Step into the cause side of your life and really go for what you want.

At the end of the day I can only be your tour guide. I have done everything I can to get you motivated to start a new, healthier life. It's up to you to make those changes, knowing that if you do so a bright future lies ahead for you. What's incredible is that simply by deciding to change the way you live your life you can transform your destiny in an instant. The only way to predict your future is to take control of it now and live your life as you were meant to – happy, fit, healthy and free. Take my words with you on your journey and know that I'm rooting for you. Here's to your well-being, good health and a deeper joy in living your life.

What are you waiting for? Just do it!

Going Further

The NLP techniques you have learned in this book can be applied to any area of your life, not just weight loss. So if you've enjoyed this programme and would like to go further with NLP, and train with me personally, here is a list of the courses run by my company, The Change Corporation:

2-DAY PROGRAMME: WEIGHT LOSS WITH NLP

This programme teaches you the techniques used in this book. You will practise the exercises and get your own weight-loss buddy.

This seminar is also available for organisations that wish to promote well-being and healthy eating, thereby reducing sickness levels among employees.

AGE WITH ATTITUDE™

This is a unique personal development programme for mid-life women, and it's the first of its kind. It's a ten-month journey spread across four events, with coaching and assistance in between each event to help keep you on track to achieve your goals. You work with other like-minded women who will support and inspire you to create the life you want.

BREAKTHROUGH COACHING

We offer a fast-track way of dealing with long-term limiting patterns of behaviour. We work intensively together for one day to resolve a particular issue and then combine this with follow-up assistance.

7-DAY FAST TRACK NLP PRACTITIONER, PRACTITIONER OF TIME LINE THERAPY™ AND PRACTITIONER OF HYPNOTHERAPY

You will learn how to use NLP techniques to transform your own life and help others. Our Practitioner programme allows you to become a Certified Practitioner of NLP in seven days. We do this by utilising pre-study CDs that you will then be able to use long after the training has finished as a useful refresher. You will also study to become a Practitioner of Time Line Therapy™ and a Practitioner of Hypnosis.

14-DAY FAST TRACK NLP MASTER PRACTITIONER, MASTER PRACTITIONER OF TIME LINE THERAPY™ AND MASTER HYPNOTIST

Our Master Practitioner programme will not only enable you to take your practitioner skills to a mastery level, but will also teach you many advanced techniques. On this course you will have the opportunity to become a Master Practitioner of Time Line Therapy™ and a Master Hypnotist. This programme also has a pre-study component.

FREE BUDDY SERVICE

This service is designed to 'buddy' readers of my books so they have someone with whom they can work together to achieve their outcomes. All you have to do is email or call us, and we'll let you know if we have anyone available to work with you. We put you in touch and then it's over to you.

If you would like more information on NLP or any of the courses available from The Change Corporation, send an email to info@thechangecorporation.com or visit our websites www.thechangecorporation.com, www.lindseyagness.com, www.agewithattitude.co.uk

Bibliography

Agness, Lindsey, *Change Your Life with NLP*, Prentice Hall Life, 2008.

Agness, Lindsey, *Still 25 Inside*, Rodale, 2010.

Brown, Derren, *Tricks of the mind*, Channel 4 Books, 2007.

Byrne, Rhonda, *The Secret*, Simon & Schuster Ltd, 2006.

Csikszentmihalyi, Mihaly, *Flow*, Rider Group, 2002.

Dooley, Mike, *Choose Them Wisely: Thoughts Become Things*, Beyond Words Publishing, 2010.

Dylan, Peggy, *Femme Vital!*, Ladybug Pr, 2009.

Glenville, Marilyn, *Fat Around the Middle*, Kyle Cathie, 2006.

Grinder, John & Bostic St. Clair, Carmen, *Whispering in the Wind*, J & C Enterprises, 2001.

James, Tad & Woodsmall, Wyatt, *Time Line Therapy and the Basis of Personality*, Meta Publications, 1989.

Knight, Sue, *NLP at Work*, Nicholas Brealey Publishing, 2004.

McKenna, Paul, *I Can Make You Thin*, Bantam Publishers, 2005.

Peer, Marissa, *You Can Be Thin*, Sphere, 2008.

Notes

CHAPTER 1:

Nearly 60 per cent of all adults want to lose weight ...
Gallop Poll, 2006.

CHAPTER 2:

Obesity has grown 400 per cent in the last 25 years ...
House of Commons Health Committee Report 'Obesity'
third report of session 2003–2004 volume 1, 10.05.04.

*Obesity will soon pass smoking as the number one cause
of premature death* ... House of Commons Health
Committee Report 'Obesity' third report of session 2003–
2004 volume 1, 10.05.04.

*For the first time in 100 years today's generation of children
will have a shorter life expectancy* ... House of Commons
Health Committee Report 'Obesity', third report of session
2003–2004 volume 1, 10.05.04.

*The UK is the country with the third highest obesity rate in
the world* ... Worldwide Obesity Figures. OECD Health
Data, 2005.

Thirdly, our lifestyles have become more sedentary than those of our parents and grandparents . . . House of Commons Health Committee Report 'Obesity' third report of session 2003–2004 volume 1, 10.05.04.

My BMI . . . Article 'Losing fat vs. losing weight', by Lucy Fry, *Women's Fitness Magazine*, May 2010.

Hip-to-waist ratio . . . Adapted with permission from *Fat Around the Middle* by Marilyn Glenville.

CHAPTER 4:

Exercise 9: This exercise is adapted from a similar one used by Nikki Owen in her workshop 'An Audience with Charisma' – used with permission. www.audiencewithcharisma.com.

CHAPTER 6:

What not to eat . . . Article 'The rise and fall of Sunny Delight' by Jennifer Clayton, *BBC News* 03.12.03.

Here are some typical calorific values of wine, beer and spirits . . . www.nutracheck.co.uk.

CHAPTER 7:

How to regulate your blood sugar . . . Article 'How to regulate your blood sugar' by Amanda Ursell, *The Times*, 03.08.08.

CHAPTER 8:

Benefits of regular exercise . . . www.healthinfo@bupa.com.

CONCLUSION:

Final tips ... Article 'Dieting for the boys' by Bruce Byron, Axa PPP Healthcare Magazine, Summer 2010.

Acknowledgements

To my parents, who are always there for me.

To my amazing children Sophie and Oliver for supporting me in all my endeavours.

To Jonny, who brightens up my universe.

To Caz, who keeps everything going at The Change Corporation.

To the members of the control group. Thanks for your commitment.

To my agents Jane and Jennifer, who keep me in exciting new projects.

To my editors at Rodale, Cindy and Lorraine, and everyone else who made the book happen.

To all my clients, who provide me with the questions, ideas and answers.